I Married a Psychic

50 Essential Life and Love Lessons I Learned
Being Married to a Psychic Medium

Mary-Frances Makichen

ISBN: 978-1-7372547-6-8 paperback

For Walter, who loved and taught me well.

ACKNOWLEDGEMENTS

To my brother, Patrick, thank you for your encouragement and for introducing me to the Lucky Duck Shut Up and Write group. The Shut Up and Write group helped me sit down and actually write this book. Thank you to all the friends I've made on IG who were so enthusiastic in their support of this book. Deep gratitude to the friends who continue to truly be there for me—you know who you are.

Special thanks to my editor, Savannah Guthrie, who was wonderfully supportive.

Lastly, I am grateful and thankful for the handful of knowledgeable, ethical and kind teachers and mentors who have helped me along this journey of life.

TABLE OF CONTENTS

INTRODUCTION

Yes, I was married to a psychic. Walter Makichen was a rather brilliant and successful one, too. Though his name might not be familiar to you, he worked for close to thirty years—mostly from referrals. He never advertised, but people always seemed to find him. If you're uncomfortable with the word psychic, I understand. A small part of me wondered what would happen when we started to live together. Would the curtain get pulled back and I'd find out it was all a scam? Nope, that was not what happened because he was the real deal. One of the things I loved about Walter was that while he was a psychic who ran a meditation center, he was also just a guy from Philly. He was a unique mix of spiritual philosopher, psychic medium, and street-smart, die-hard Phillies fan.

People generally had a couple of different reactions to meeting my husband. Many people were really nervous around him. They worried about what he would see about them, what secrets he might dig up. They were wary. Other people were fascinated by him and wanted to know *everything*. I was often asked what it *was like* to be married to a psychic?

I'm not sure what people thought, but here's what I

think they imagined. In the mornings, we wake up gazing into each other's eyes, staring into the depths of each other's souls. As he reaches over and tucks a strand of hair behind my ear he says, "I see you, my love, in this lifetime and all the others." Then we roll out of bed and head immediately to our meditation cushions where we face each other with arms outstretched as we touch the other's heart chakra. He calls in the spirits all around us and gives me insight into what I can expect to encounter throughout my day. Each morning, I get a short, private mini-reading just for me about my karma and my akashic records, and then a soulful bout of deeply moving tantric sex.

I can't tell you how much I wish Walter were still alive to read that paragraph. He'd shake his head and laugh for a while. Here's a little dose of reality. He stayed up really late. He did that because he liked the quiet. Not just the quiet of this world at night, but he would also always say that the astral plane and world of energy in general cleared out. Everything got quiet and less crowded then. It was easier to see things clairvoyantly and work with energy. On the other hand, I'm not much of a night owl. We rarely went to bed at the same time, and I was always up at least a few hours before him. When he'd get up in the morning, the first thing he'd want was a latte. Every day, I used our little espresso maker to make him one. *Every day.* And yet some mornings, when the service wasn't fast enough, he'd ask, "Are you going to make me a latte today?" I would roll my eyes, laugh, and say, "When have I not made you one?" or "The service isn't fast enough this morning, huh?" It was one of our long-standing "married couple" conversations and I loved it. Then he would slowly wake up while I randomly read either emails or headlines to him. I'm not sure if he really liked me doing that or not, but he indulged me… and that was our morning routine.

So far, I haven't run across another clairvoyant who is as clear or as talented as Walter was. I'm not just saying that because I was married to him. Ask anyone he ever helped with a reading or class. He was amazing at what he did. I had the privilege of knowing him for just over twenty years before he died. During most of those years, we worked side-by-side nearly 24/7. Before he got sick, he used to joke that he and I spent more time together than couples who were married twice as long. To this day, I'm so grateful for that time.

Being married to Walter was an adventure. I learned so much by watching him work, asking questions, and really listening. Despite the earlier joke about what it was like to be married to him, there were times that it might be exactly what you imagine. Because he was such a consistently open channel, our house was filled with spirits and ghosts who were attracted to his work. I distinctly remember one morning when he got up and asked me, "Did the monster in the house wake you up last night?" Even I was a bit taken aback. "The what?" I asked. He went on to explain that there'd been an unwelcome wild energy being that he'd had to throw out of the house. From his point of view, the whole thing had been noisy. He couldn't believe I'd slept through it. So, yeah, that kind of stuff definitely happened.

For a long time, I wanted to write a book that shared all the things I learned from Walter—both the man and the psychic. But every time I tried, it became this heavy book about spiritual pathways and awareness. It just didn't come together. Always, in the back of my mind, I'd hear a voice whisper, "Write 'I married a psychic'," and I'd smile briefly before turning to the more "serious" spiritual work I thought I should share. Then one day, I'm not sure what happened, but I sat down and all the topics for this book came pouring out of me—throughout one afternoon and evening. So, here we are.

Everything I could think of that I learned from being married to a psychic is broken down into bite-size pieces of wisdom. Some of them are practical while others are mystical or even whimsical.

I hope this book brings a smile to your face, makes you laugh, makes you think, and, in general, gives you the feels. Walter lives on in my heart always.

1

GIVE YOURSELF PERMISSION

HAVE YOU EVER noticed that when we think we don't know what to do in our lives, we turn to others for guidance? I've found for myself, and in working with other people, that often what we're really looking for is someone to tell us "it's okay." We want someone to give us permission to move in the direction where we already know we want to go.

I'll let you in on a *big* not-so-secret secret. When we seek out psychics, coaches, or mentors, 95 percent of the time what we're truly looking for is permission to make the change we want to make. I watched Walter do this constantly for people. I remember when we first met and I started working with him. One day at the end of a reading, he told me I could be a writer and probably would be one. I was shocked. I'd always loved to write but it had never occurred to me that I could be a writer, let alone a paid one. All it took was one person telling me I could do it, one person putting that idea in my mind and saying, "Yes, you." He gave me permission and I ran with it.

For some reason, we humans need someone to see something in us first—maybe a longing or a talent—and believe in our ability, for us to trust something is possible. Not all the time, of course, but we often look for a source outside ourselves to say, "Yes, go for it!" I think it's part of our change process, knowing we want to change and seeking out the people who can help us. We borrow their belief in us until we're strong and secure enough to believe in ourselves. There's nothing wrong with that at all.

Consider giving yourself permission—permission to dream big, to change, to be something entirely different, to nurture that secret longing you have. Stop thinking to yourself, "Oh, other people can do that, but I can't." Of course you can. Be bold and don't wait for someone else to give you permission. Take authority over who you want to be and what you want to do.

THE LESSON

You don't need other people to give you permission to live your truth and dare greatly.

THE PRACTICE

Life is one big experiment and adventure. Can you choose one thing in your life you would normally ask for other people's opinions on before moving forward? Instead of waiting for someone else to validate your thoughts and feelings, can you let yourself step forward and just start? Don't ask, just do. You don't have to change your whole life. Start small. Take that dance class you always wanted to take, color your hair green, start the podcast you've had in the back of your mind. Today, just say yes to one thing you want to do, instead of no.

WHAT HELPS

Somewhere along the way, we decided a certain path wasn't for us. "Oh, I can't be a writer," or "Who do I think I am to start my own business?" Whatever it is you think isn't for you but you secretly want to do, why not just try doing it and see what happens?

2

"I SEE DEAD PEOPLE"
IS A REAL THING

I GET IT. Some of you are believers, some of you aren't sure, and the rest of you think this is wacky. Whichever category you fall into, all I can do is share some of my own experiences. Living with a clairvoyant medium meant there was a certain flow of spirits through our house all the time. I didn't realize until after Walter died that the flow was really because of him. On some level, the work he did as a medium created an opening for spirits to find our house in a way that doesn't happen to me now. It was never scary, there were never any cold spots, and pieces of furniture didn't move around our house. I'm not saying those things don't occur. I'm saying that in our house, Walter had established very strong boundaries. Think of it this way: it's as if we were always entertaining and a lot of different people stopped by to say hello all the time.

I remember one day I glanced over at the kitchen table. I'd gotten a new felted purse that looked like something out of the 1950s. My purse was on the table, and sitting right by it in one of the kitchen chairs was a little old lady. She looked like she was right out of the 1950s, too, down to the cute little hat she was wearing. She was sitting super close to my purse and looked almost like she was holding it. I turned to Walter and said, "Is there a little old lady sitting next to my purse?" He busted up laughing. "Yeah, she really likes your purse." I laughed, shrugged my shoulders, and went about my business for the day. When you're married to a psychic medium, that kind of stuff is par for the course.

At the request of a loved one, Walter would help people pass over to wherever they were headed. That place was different for everyone. Walter believed in reincarnation. In his experience, people's thoughts about death affected what they first experienced when they died. After that, he believed there was a review of life that happened before they moved on.

From watching Walter do this work, I became acquainted with the idea of people not knowing they're dead, especially if someone's death is sudden or traumatic. They may roam around confused, trying to figure out what's happening. I can't tell you I understand how it all works. I'm not sure what I think happens after we die. That's something I really won't know until it happens to me. Just in case there is an afterlife, I've put it firmly in my mind that Walter will be there waiting for me. When I go into the white light, I expect to see him again.

THE LESSON

It may seem like our time here is infinite, but it really isn't. Don't leave anything unsaid or undone with those you love.

Don't wait to live your life. If you want to travel, don't wait for the perfect partner to travel with you. Just go now. Whatever you're waiting for to live your life, stop waiting and get busy living. If you feel stuck, ask for help and be proactive in seeking out what you need to move forward.

THE PRACTICE

We get so caught up in all the doings of our lives that it's as if we are in a dream, not quite there. We are busy trying to get to the next moment and the one after that instead of being in this snippet of time. See if you can fit in some moments throughout the day when you stop everything and just take a couple of deep breaths. Let yourself catch up to the moment you're in.

WHAT HELPS

Quiet time, being out in nature, and meditation can help you remember that you are a part of something larger than yourself. Practice being intentional with your attention and time.

3

YOU DON'T NEED ANYONE'S APPROVAL TO LIVE THE LIFE YOU WANT

WALTER'S GRANDPARENTS WERE immigrants. His mother's side of the family was from Italy, while his father's side was from Ukraine. His parents were first generation Americans and neither one had gone to a four-year college. Originally, Walter had planned on being an English professor. He was attending UC Berkeley and working toward his PhD when life took him in a very different direction. During that time, he started to understand his own abilities. He realized he'd seen energy and auras all his life. He also became confident in his ability to connect with people who had died, spirit guides, and reading energy clairvoyantly.

As you can imagine, when he told his working class parents that he was dropping out of school to become a clairvoyant and start a meditation center, they were not pleased. His dad, in particular, had a hard time with it. Walter and his father loved each other a lot but they had an uneasy relationship. His father didn't approve of or understand Walter's choices, and Walter craved his dad's approval. I'm not entirely sure of the timing, but I believe Walter was in his mid-20s, home in Philadelphia for a visit, when he and his dad had another fight about his future. In that moment, Walter realized he had to stop wanting his father's approval. He realized that, to live the life he wanted to live, he had to let go of ever wanting *anyone's* approval. The only person's opinion that mattered was his own. In all the time I knew him, I never once saw him waver from that.

When we want someone to approve of something we're doing, we're essentially giving them power over our actions. We're also, to some degree, making them responsible for our decisions. After all, we count on their approval to confirm that what we're doing is okay or that we're on the right path. Walter realized wanting that approval wasn't fair to himself or his dad. Sometimes, the people we most want approval from just can't give it to us, for whatever reason. Then we're angry or annoyed with them because they haven't given us what we thought we needed to move forward, make a decision, or live a certain way. As soon as Walter let go of wanting his dad's approval, a great weight was lifted. Walter went on to be highly successful and his dad eventually respected what his son had created.

THE LESSON

Part of the journey of life is realizing you don't need anyone's approval to be who you want to be and to live how you want to live.

THE PRACTICE

Notice who you seek out for validation when you need to make a decision. Who in your life do you want to make "happy" with your choices and lifestyle? Looking for approval from others can be an unconscious action. Do you want to be thought of in a certain way? If so, ask yourself: by whom? Whoever that is, is someone you may be looking to for approval. One of the first steps you can take is to see where you want approval in your life. Acknowledge it's there and don't judge it. Instead, let yourself begin to become more aware of how it affects you.

WHAT HELPS

Be your biggest supporter and believe in yourself. Give yourself authority over your own life. Give to yourself what others may not or will not be able to give you.

4

BE THE AUTHORITY OVER
YOUR OWN LIFE

WHO HAS AUTHORITY in your life? Walter used to say that if you have a newborn in your home, they are the authority. Why? Because your life and attention are completely given over to the care and needs of that newborn. New parents completely change their everyday lives and habits to care for them. There isn't anything they wouldn't do to take care of that baby.

Authority is an interesting word. For some, it has a negative connotation. In this instance, think of it in terms of who truly has the power to shape your life. We often unconsciously give authority over certain aspects of our lives to others.

For instance, in domestic relationships, one person may take on all the finances. The partner who doesn't want anything to do with the finances lets go of their authority over that area. They may not know the true state of their financial situation unless they actively pin their partner down about where things are. Ceding authority isn't necessarily a bad thing. It's very common to give authority over parts of our lives to someone else. It only becomes an issue when we do it unconsciously, without any thought of why we're doing it. Maybe you unconsciously want your partner to manage all the finances because you have a lot of issues around money. As long as your partner is willing to take this on and is good at it, ceding the authority works out. It's usually when the relationship breaks up or if the partner gets tired of being the one in charge that it becomes clear we gave this authority or power away without a lot of thought.

I think the easiest way to understand this is to ask yourself: who has the authority to make me change my life? As Walter said, if you're a new parent, your baby has the authority to make you change your life and habits. If you work for someone else, then your boss has the authority to make changes to your schedule and you will go along with it. We temporarily give our work managers authority over our schedules when we work for them.

The bigger question comes when we want to do something for ourselves, like change a habit. Maybe we want to find a new job or move someplace new. Do we have enough authority within ourselves to make changes once we decide on them? If we say we're going to do something for ourselves, are we able to keep our word? For many people, that inner authority gets developed a little bit at a time. It's often prompted by a serious shock in our lives, like a divorce or job loss. It's during times of crisis that we see what we have authority over in our lives. This exchange of authority with others isn't good or bad and it's very normal. What's most important is that we are aware of the exchange. The authority we have over our lives also changes over time, along with our circumstances and relationships.

THE LESSON

Be aware of who and what has the authority to shape your life. It can be easy to hand over authority on certain areas of our lives to someone else. That's neither bad nor good. What we do want is to understand where we do it and why.

THE PRACTICE

Sometimes, we unconsciously or inadvertently give someone else power over aspects of our lives, like finances, where we live, who we interact with, or even how we dress. Look at one area of your life where you may have given your power away and consider how to call it back. Just like anything we learn in life, this is a skill that you practice bit by bit. Ultimately, you are showing yourself that when you make a promise to yourself, you will keep it.

WHAT HELPS

There is much in this world that we cannot control, such as systems and governments that shape our outer lives, but we can all have inner authority over ourselves. We can decide what things we put our time and attention toward. We can decide who we trust and how we want to direct our lives. It's important to be aware of the authority we have in our lives and feel secure enough to take on that responsibility for ourselves.

5

TRUST YOURSELF TO FIND
WHAT'S NEEDED

ONE OF THE coolest things about being married to Walter was watching how he approached life. We all face the mundane tasks of life. In fact, the logistics of living in this world take up much of our lives. We are faced with all the typical decisions, like where we should live or what job we should have. Watching how Walter worked with the energy of the very common logistics of living in this world always interested me.

There are a few specific tools he used often throughout our relationship. When looking at a situation that needed some kind of action or decision, Walter would meditate and simply ask that anything needing to be revealed or uncovered about the decision-making process be brought to light in some way. Walter meditated every night, and part of that time he would hold the space for this type of energy work. He rarely asked what he should do, or for a definitive answer. I saw this approach work time and time again, and it's something I adopted, as well. Behind this approach is trusting everything we need to navigate our lives will present itself, as needed and as appropriate, for us to take action.

The other tool Walter often used was working subconsciously on an issue while he slept. Many times, before going to bed, he would intentionally hold a question or concern he was analyzing and ask for it to be worked on during the night. Walter trusted that his subconscious would find the idea or next piece of the puzzle he needed. He also stayed attentive and open to information and answers coming to him from all kinds of unexpected places and sources.

No matter what method he used, there was always a trust that he was never alone. Walter believed that in an interconnected universe he was part of a greater force and wholeness, and that wholeness was part of him.

THE LESSON

Trust that when you hold attention on a question or issue and ask for help that it will be given. You will find what you need.

THE PRACTICE

We get swept away by the busyness of our lives and often forget to hold a space to ask for help. It can be even more difficult to get past our own anxiety and anxiousness to hold a space that lets us see what is being revealed and for information that's needed to find us. If you already have a meditation practice, make asking for help a part of it. If you don't have a practice, consider setting aside time to sit quietly and hold space to ask for help. It truly can be just a few minutes, as often as you like, throughout the week.

WHAT HELPS

It is often just the act of acknowledging our need for help that allows us to see the resources we already have gathered around us. Be purposeful and intentional when it comes to asking for help. You don't have to find the answers by yourself.

6

LET YOUR SUBCONSCIOUS WORK ON A PROBLEM WHILE YOU SLEEP

You MAY BE thinking, "Doesn't our subconscious normally work through the events of our day while we're asleep?" Yes, but as mentioned in the previous chapter, there's also a way we can be intentional about this process. Thomas Edison said, "Never go to sleep without a request to your subconscious." Walter was an expert when it came to finding solutions while he slept.

Making a request to the subconscious is something you can easily do. Try it and see what happens. I was always amazed at how well this process worked for Walter. With a bit of practice, perseverance, and attention, anyone can successfully apply this methodology. Instead of gnawing on a problem, intentionally let it go from your conscious mind. This is the process that happens when we stop focusing on an issue, and suddenly an answer pops into our heads while we're in the shower or exercising. Trust that the answer will come when and how it needs to come. Consider keeping a notebook by your bed. Jot down your thoughts after waking up but before you engage with the world (e.g. your phone, news, social media, email, etc.). Recording this free flow of your waking thoughts before any other elements are introduced to your mind is an important part of this process.

What I've observed the most about this is that it opens us up to a world of possibilities. Maybe we don't get a direct answer, but suddenly, someone we know introduces us to a new connection and they're able to offer the insight or information we need. If you keep track of the requests you make to your subconscious over time, you can go back and see how things changed after the fact. We may not even realize something has shifted and that we've been heading in a new direction until enough time has passed. Then we're able to see the road our subconscious took us on *after* we made the formal request for help. Experiment and see what happens.

THE LESSON

Your subconscious is always working, even while you sleep. Give it something specific to ponder while your conscious mind is out of the way.

THE PRACTICE

Before you go to sleep, take some time to think about your challenges. Get specific about what issues you're looking for help with. Keep a notebook near your bed and write it all down. Ask your subconscious to connect with the answer, or the next step you need to take, during your sleep. When you wake, take more notes about any dreams you remember or whatever comes to mind. Don't worry if an exact answer isn't there. You can go back through the thoughts or dreams you've jotted down later and see if they spark any understanding or creative direction for you.

WHAT HELPS

Do the practice more than once. Have fun with it. Use it to keep your creativity flowing, and be open to help coming from all different sources. Trust yourself to bring forth what you need and to find the next step to take.

7

MAKE SMALL ACTS OF FAITH
IN YOURSELF EVERY DAY

MAKING SMALL ACTS of faith in myself was something that arose from one of the first series of reading work I did with Walter. He talked about the importance of making small, daily acts of faith in ourselves. What does that mean? It varies for each of us and spans the different parts of our lives. To make change or create the kind of life you want, big resets aren't necessarily needed. Instead, the consistency of small acts over time makes a difference.

A small act of faith could be something like:

- Meditating for five minutes
- Exercising for ten minutes
- Writing for ten minutes
- Organizing your space five minutes every day
- Taking an online class that you watch in ten-minute intervals

These are examples of things you can put a bit of time

into, if not daily, then almost daily. It's definitely not "I'm going to sit down and meditate for an hour every day," or "I'm going to watch online classes for three hours every night." Those aren't small, manageable things; those are big, intimidating things.

As human beings, we tend to like extremes, the highs and lows. Consistency is not as exciting as pulling all-nighters several times a week and running on fumes and coffee. What we do know about being successful is that consistency over time is extremely important. Walter looked at taking on small practices as training for taking on bigger challenges. Start with something doable, that you can be successful with, and then build on that energy. This type of action helps you learn to trust yourself. If you say you're going to do something, will you do it? Do you have authority over yourself and your actions? When you decide to make small acts of faith in yourself, one of the things you gain is confidence in your efforts.

I have to tell you, too, that there is a certain magic that happens when you get to the place in your life where you say you will do something and you do it. Not for other people, but for yourself. I saw this with Walter constantly. There was an almost instant momentum that happened when he decided to do something because he knew he could trust his word and it would happen. This starts by making small acts of faith in yourself every day. Part of the reason these acts must be reasonable and doable is you will meet your own resistance. Accomplishing a small, doable effort makes the resistance much more manageable to overcome than if we say, "Okay, today I'm going to change everything in my life." The inner pushback we encounter is equal to the energy of our effort. This is why it's so important to make small acts of faith in ourselves. They are the foundation we need to trust ourselves and take our word to as golden.

THE LESSON

Having authority over our own lives starts with being able to trust that we will do what we say we will for ourselves.

THE PRACTICE

Small acts of faith in ourselves are just that. Start with the smallest, most manageable action you can think of. Set yourself up for success—not failure—even if a part of you says, "Well, that's so small, of course I can do that!" Don't overthink it. Just make that small act of faith in yourself every day for a week or two and then see where you are. Plan for resistance. Know it will appear in many guises, learn to recognize it, and move forward anyway with as much grace as you can muster.

WHAT HELPS

It's often easier to be accountable to other people rather than to ourselves. We have a million reasons why we couldn't do what we said we would when it comes to ourselves and our goals. Resistance is a very real force in our lives. It will always be there. Learn to work with it to your benefit with skill, acceptance, discipline, and intention.

8.

GUARDIAN ANGELS ARE
A REAL THING

WALTER WORKED CLOSELY with angels and the angelic realm in general. So yes, I believe in angels. One of the most interesting things about angels that I learned from Walter is they have no sense of individualism or an "I." When they speak, it is always from a place of "we", and they have no sense of separation. My understanding is the purpose of angels is to help us feel connected, to help us always feel the familiarity—the family—that is the universe.

Angels interact with our lives in different ways. One is that they guard our life pathway. At crucial points in your life, they may be the whisper you hear to take the right fork in the road instead of the left. They help safeguard your path in this life if intervention is necessary.

Another kind of interaction occurs through prayer. When we pray out of a sense of loneliness and isolation, no matter to whom, we will often receive an angelic response. They step in to remind us there's more to the universe than singularity. Angels simply respond to a person's need to feel connected. The angelic realm is all about interconnectedness.

You may think this is odd, but guardian angels look after animals as well. Walter and I had many pets together—dogs, cats, and parrots. Walter would send prayers out for angels to watch over any animal that was ill. He'd also pray they'd be safe if we were traveling and away from them for a while. These simple prayers asking angels to keep our pets safe and well brought me a definite sense of comfort and well-being.

Guardian angels do not belong to any one religious or spiritual practice. The angelic realm is an equal opportunity response team. If you feel alone or you wonder if there isn't more to life than you can see or feel, ask an angel for help. In a realm focused on the idea of "we" and being connected, asking for help is not considered a weakness, it's considered a reality. Maybe heaven is not feeling separate but instead truly understanding that we're all connected.

THE LESSON

We are all connected to each other and the universe. Another way to say it is we are all a part of a larger wholeness.

THE PRACTICE

Help, in its many different forms, is always all around us. We often forget to actually ask for help. If it's difficult for you to remember to ask for it, think about putting a reminder note up where you'll see it every day. It can say something like, "Help is always around me" or "Don't be afraid to ask for what I need." If you're not the sort to pray, then reach out to others. If you are the sort to pray, ask your guardian angels for help. You don't need any special prayer. Keep it simple and let it come from your heart.

WHAT HELPS

It can be easy to forget we are more than our bodies or personalities. Each of us is connected to something sacred that we can catch glimpses of through prayer, meditation, or quiet moments. In this connection, we are never alone.

9.

MEDITATION PRACTICE
PROVIDES A REFUGE

THERE ARE MANY well documented benefits to meditating. We know it enhances our overall sense of well-being, lowers stress levels, and improves our focus. After Walter died, I discovered a regular meditation practice can also be a refuge, a safe space to return to over and over again.

The first year after Walter's death, I tried to meditate, hoping it would help me get through my grief. I would sit down in front of the little altar I'd made, take a couple of breaths, and then instantly break into tears. This happened repeatedly during that first year. Looking back, I'm surprised I kept trying, because the experience felt awful. It didn't fill me with a sense of comfort. It felt ugly, jagged, and raw. Yet for some reason, I kept going back to it. Not every day but at least a couple of times a week. Over time, it happened: sitting down to meditate and not crying. Instead, I would sit and breathe, listening to the sound of my breath. I chanted, prayed, and asked for help from something higher so I could move forward.

The space I returned to a few times every week—a square of hardwood floor covered by a seat cushion—became my sacred space. It could have been any spot anywhere I sat over time. What made it sacred was the intention I brought to it. I listened to my breath, eyes closed, and looked within for compassion. I searched for the new awareness of who I was in these changed circumstances. This small spot on the hardwood floor provided a steady place for me to practice attention and awareness in the wake of a terrible loss.

I sat and I breathed. The longer I did, the more something miraculous began to take shape. Every time I sat and opened to the moment in front of me, I was creating a refuge for myself. An inner space I could return to again and again. A sacred place where I experienced my humanness and divinity at the same time. It's always there and I am always practicing. I am always starting again because in every moment I change, as does the world around me.

THE LESSON

The consistent practice of awareness through meditation creates a sacred inner refuge you can always carry with you.

THE PRACTICE

When it comes to meditation, start small. So small you feel it's ridiculous, and then repeat it as often as possible. Create a goal so manageable that the only option is for you to succeed.

For example, you could meditate for two to five minutes, three times a week, before the kids get up in the morning or at night after the busyness of the day is over. As the habit takes shape you can go for longer periods. Understand that meditation is called a practice because it is. There's no perfect way to do it. Some days, meditation will be magical while other days it will feel like a struggle. Expect periods when your practice will wane a bit, but know your attention and breath will always welcome you back without question.

WHAT HELPS

Our lives are busy, and resistance is real. It can be difficult to make time to sit quietly and cultivate awareness through meditation. Using tools like apps and guided meditations can help make it easier.

10.

EVERYTHING WORKS
SOME OF THE TIME

"EVERYTHING WORKS SOME of the time" was one of Walter's all-time favorite sayings. It may come off as flippant, but there's some deep truth in this statement that I return to all the time. I really don't know how this phrase came about. I can't track it back to any particular class or talk. I can tell you Walter worked with thousands of people throughout his life. He had many strategies in his toolbox to help people. Through the course of his work, he saw that life, healing, and spirituality are not one-size-fits-all propositions.

Walter was really good at meeting people where they were, not where he was. He knew energy was always changing. We're always changing. Our energy systems, our breath, our emotions, even the cells in our bodies are always changing. We may do something ninety-nine times and have it work, and then we hit 100 and it no longer works the same way. I've come to think of this phrase as the rallying cry for not giving up. It speaks to the idea that we may need to change what we're doing and try different things until we figure out what resonates right now. "Everything works some of the time" reminds us not to get caught up in what worked in the past.

Most of the time, meditation helps me in many different ways. It usually leaves me feeling centered, focused, and calm. Then there are times when it has the completely opposite effect on me. I didn't do anything different from the day before or the day before that, but the outcome is completely different. No matter what I do as I try to meditate, I'll find myself feeling more and more agitated. I can try to trace it back to a specific thought or emotion. I can try to make myself breathe through it, but it just doesn't work. This doesn't happen very often, but when it does, oh boy, I have to do something else like getting up and taking a walk. This doesn't mean I give up on meditation. It just means that in an ever-changing world, being flexible and open to what's needed in the present moment is a good strategy.

People are creatures of habit and we can cling stubbornly to the things we're comfortable with, the things in our lives that are tried and true. We may keep trying to make something work long after it's stopped working. It's as if we're repeatedly trying to cram a square peg into a triangular hole that used to be square. We shake our heads and wonder why it's not working, instead of trying something new.

THE LESSON

Lives change, circumstances change, we change. What worked for us at one point in our lives may not work for us at another. A medical treatment that works for one person may not work for someone with the same issues. Everything works some of the time.

THE PRACTICE

If something is no longer serving you, can you let it go? Can you pay attention to what you need at this moment instead of what previously worked for you? Don't give up if what used to work isn't working now. Keep trying. Journaling is a great way to keep track of how changes in approach affect your outcomes. Over time, you'll be able to see patterns emerge that will help you understand what resonates and what no longer works for you.

WHAT HELPS

Be open and flexible to the possibilities around you. Sometimes, you'll find only a minor adjustment is necessary. Other times, your life may require a completely new approach.

11.

TALKING CAN DILUTE THE ENERGY OF SOMETHING YOU'RE TRYING TO CREATE

IN MY LATE twenties, I was an expert at diluting the energy of an idea. I'm sure Walter watched me do this often. I remember when I would get excited about something I wanted to do, and instead of taking action toward the goal itself, I would just talk about it to different people. I wanted to share my idea, see what other people thought about it, and really roll it around in my head… all before I actually started.

Once in a reading, Walter told me I ran the yellowest yellow he'd ever seen. Yellow is the color of the third chakra—an energy point in the body located in the solar plexus. It's considered the chakra that takes action and puts our will out into the world. He said I would send action energy up to my sixth chakra (an energy point located in the space between the eyebrows) and think about it until I had drained all the color, all the action, out of it. Walter acted differently. He was definitely a thinker, but he kept many things to himself or would only share them with one or two people close to him. When he was ready to act, he did. More than once when I asked him about talking something through or sharing what he was doing with other people, he'd just shake his head and say no. He wanted to build on the energy of his idea or project by putting his energy into its creation. Walter often said he'd rather be the person who created things other people judged or criticized instead of being a critic of other people's work.

It's easy to mistake talking about creating something or sharing an idea as taking action. There's a difference, though, between thinking, talking, and doing. We may think talking about something is the first step to action. However, the way to take action is to act. When we keep talking about something we want to create without starting it, we can also talk ourselves out of what we want to do. When we tell a lot of people about our idea, their reactions or opinions may slowly drain our enthusiasm or belief in what we want to create.

However we choose to run our creative energy in this world, we must protect our creation. Don't dilute the energy of what you want to create by chewing on it until all the flavor is gone. Don't talk endlessly about what you want to do. Just start. Let the energy build. Put your energy into acting and creating something that only you can.

THE LESSON

"To everything there is a season, and a time to every purpose under the heaven... a time to keep silent and a time to speak..." Ecclesiastes 3:1 *New American Standard Bible.*

This quote is perfect because there is a time to keep

silent and a time to speak. When we are looking at making a change or creating something new, we can talk it to death before we act. Don't suck all the juicy energy out of a project by talking about it endlessly while not doing much else.

THE PRACTICE

Believe in yourself and in what you're doing. Know that if you're creating something, it may take several iterations to get to where you're going. Grab an adhesive note or index card and write down all the reasons you want to move forward with your idea, project, or direction. Also write down what this project means to you and list all the important whys. Keep these notes around you, and review them as often as you need to keep focused and remember why you began in the first place.

WHAT HELPS

As excited as you may be about something you want to do or create, you should also be aware of whom you want to share with and why. There's nothing wrong with looking for feedback or a sounding board, but strive to be intentional and deliberate about whom you choose to tell and how much telling you do versus how much action you take. Be fiercely protective of what you're working on. Negative voices come from both outside and inside of us. Understand that in some ways, you are taking on the practice of coming back to your work no matter how many times you lose faith or focus in what you're doing.

12.

SOME WORDS CAN NEVER BE UNSAID, SOME LINES SHOULDN'T BE CROSSED

WALTER AND I agreed early in our relationship to be mindful of how and what we would say to each other during any disagreements we had. Put two Aries in a relationship and things can get heated. So we made a commitment to being aware of how we argued with each other. I can tell you it worked well for us, but I'm not a relationship expert. Walter worked with many couples. I never asked him if this idea came out of his work or if this was something he had come to on his own.

Let's face it—relationships can be challenging. No one can push our buttons quite like a loved one can, am I right? Arguments in a primary relationship can sometimes bring out our most adolescent side. In anger and defensiveness, we may find ourselves being mean or going for what we know is our partner's vulnerable spot. Walter and I agreed we would be mindful that certain things once said couldn't be taken back—even if said while angry. Couples can forgive each other, of course, but once you put something out there, once you cross a line, things shift. We can forgive and accept apologies, but we also remember very hurtful words were said.

This is different from when a partner communicates something to us in a respectful way that makes us uncomfortable, triggering our own insecurities. Of course, this doesn't only apply to partners; any relationship, whether it's other family members or friends, must navigate this. When we're frustrated or hurt, sometimes our first instinct may be to strike back and make someone else hurt as much as we do. Obviously, this isn't a great way to operate. What Walter and I did was set ground rules for dealing with disagreements that worked for us. It was something we consciously discussed. In any relationship, especially an intimate one, there will always be times when you disagree. Planning how to approach opposing points of view can be very helpful.

THE LESSON

Remember: words have the power to hurt and heal. Choose how you approach boundaries carefully and mindfully.

THE PRACTICE

In the heat of the moment, we sometimes don't think about the long-term damage our words can inflict. When we feel hurt or defensive, we often react without thinking. In those moments, the challenge is to remember that we've made a commitment to avoid being careless or intentionally hurtful to someone else.

WHAT HELPS

Find the strategies and tools that help you argue construc-
tively in your relationships. When you feel things veering off
track, take a beat, walk around the block—whatever it takes
to cool down. Everyone is different, but find what works for
you so you don't cross lines you'll regret.

13.

BOUNDARIES ARE SELF-CARE

WHEN WE WANT other people to like us, boundaries can be challenging to establish. I remember the first time I heard Walter suggest saying "no" to someone was sometimes the most compassionate thing you could do. At that time, this was a revolutionary idea for me. Most of us don't like being told "no." It can bring up feelings of rejection and disappointment. But saying "yes" when we don't want to, when we feel uncomfortable or awkward, isn't useful either. We are responsible for taking care of ourselves by communicating what we need to others. It can take a lot of practice to ask for what we need from a calm, self-assured place instead of an exasperated and angry one.

Setting boundaries with people helps them understand you. Saying "yes" when we know we won't be able to honor the yes isn't helpful to anyone. In fact, it almost always leads to more complications and feelings of resentment. Saying "no" when you need to, directly and with compassion, is a great self-care practice. You are not responsible for someone else's response to your no. They are responsible for hearing the no, possibly asking some questions, honoring it, and then working out whatever reaction or emotions they have around being refused. It sounds simple; but when it comes to communication in any kind of relationship, having boundaries can be tricky. Communication is key to setting boundaries.

Establishing new boundaries with people can be especially challenging in ongoing relationships. When that happens, it's as if we're changing the terms of the relationship contract we have with someone. We're asking for an amendment, and this especially can cause conflict. Still, when we establish boundaries, we are valuing ourselves and acknowledging our needs. We are letting people know what interactions and behaviors we want in our lives. Boundaries are the structures we set that support everything else. As our lives and circumstances change, our boundaries may change as well.

THE LESSON

Sometimes the most compassionate thing you can do for someone is say, "No."

THE PRACTICE

Setting boundaries takes practice! Remind yourself that establishing boundaries is part of taking care of yourself and being your own advocate. If you're anticipating a difficult conversation with someone about boundaries, try these tips:

- Be mindful of when to have the conversation. While there may not be a perfect time, try to schedule it when you have the other person's full attention and emotions aren't charged.

- Beforehand, think about writing out the points you want to make and how the other person can best support you around this boundary.
- Breathe deeply and get grounded.
- If you anticipate anger and hurt feelings may come out of this discussion, ask another friend to be available to touch base with after you're done.

WHAT HELPS

It's easy to want to please other people and not rock the boat. We often don't want to deal with people's reactions when we say "no" or establish a boundary. Their reaction, if it's negative, can feel scary and overwhelming. Nevertheless, you and your emotional well-being are worth setting boundaries with others.

14.

CLEAN AND CLEAR THE ENERGY OF YOUR LIVING SPACE

DOES CLEANING AND clearing the energy of your living space make absolute sense to you or does it sound woo woo? We clean our spaces on a physical level, but did you know energy can hang around your living space too? One of the things I observed when living with Walter was how meticulous and intentional he was about energetically cleaning out our house every day. Part of this was due to his work. Walter was a channel and there were always a lot of spirits and different energies collecting and converging in our space. It may sound odd, but the corners of rooms—especially at the ceiling—collect energy. Regular, physical cleaning can help move energy along. However, it doesn't take the place of cleaning out the energy itself.

When you think about it, everything is made up of some type of energy. In our homes, some of the energies that tend to hang around the most are strong emotions. If there's been a fight, you've been depressed, or you've spent a lot of time worrying over a situation, the residue of those emotions can hang around the house. Think about the different spaces you've walked into and how you've reacted to them. You visit one person's place and the energy feels good, while someone else's might feel tense or off in some way. You are picking up the energy of not only the person, but also the energy most prevalent in the space.

Cleaning out the space is a lot like taking an eraser to a whiteboard. You wipe the slate clean so you can start fresh again. It's the same thing in your own space. Instead of being affected by yesterday's emotions and energies, let yourself create a clean slate and a fresh start. If you do much personal development or spiritual work in your space, it's especially important to keep the energy clean.

There are many different ways to clean out a space and clean out energy. Walter's favorite was working with a white spiral. In meditation, he would take a white spiral through each room, especially the corners. You can also use sage or some other cleansing herb, light it, and walk through each room and to every corner, letting the smoke clear out the energy. Other people use bowls of salt or saltwater. This is something that you can do yourself—no previous experience necessary. I've found there is something especially satisfying about cleaning the energy of your space. It's a way of intentionally letting go of what's come before and re-establishing a sense of balance and well-being.

THE LESSON

Clearing out your space on an energetic level is a good way to take care of yourself and create a fresh and peaceful space.

THE PRACTICE

If you're the kind of person who cleans their house on a certain day each week, why not add an energetic cleaning on that same day? If, like me, your cleaning schedule is more variable, you can add it to your calendar as a recurring weekly appointment. It is ideal if you can do it daily at the end of your day, but as often as you can works too. Some ways to clear your energetic space include burning sage or palo santo, or ringing bells throughout your space.

WHAT HELPS

We all have very busy lives, and this extra step can seem like just another thing to do. In the physical world, we can sometimes forget the importance and influence of the unseen world in which we also exist. Clearing out the energy of your space can create more flow and connection between the two worlds.

15.

BE WILLING TO WALK AWAY

ONE OF THE things I watched Walter embody very consistently was not needing anyone's permission or approval to do his work in this world. It's empowering to be around someone who believes in themselves and their work strongly and steadfastly. This doesn't mean he didn't compromise or try new things to see what would happen. It does mean he had faith and trust in his process and ability to manifest what he needed without giving up pieces of himself to others.

Walter held his sense of self, his boundaries, and his own power very strongly. He was never afraid to walk away from a situation if necessary. He knew that if he walked away, it wasn't the right situation for him in the first place, and what he needed or was looking for would come to him some other way. He was fearless in this regard.

I would see people struggle with his ability to walk away at times. They might be used to getting their way by using tears or some other emotional pressure that generally worked for them. While Walter was very kind and empathetic, he could also let go of relationships and situations that did not serve his life purpose. For many of us, our need to be a "nice," "good," or "understanding" person will keep us tethered to situations that drain our energy and chip away at our souls. Because Walter did not need anyone else's approval, and understood people's opinions of him were just that, he could quickly and decisively turn away from situations that were not right for him.

The ability to walk away requires both courage and awareness to see when it's appropriate to do so. It's not as if Walter walked away from things all the time. He could be very persistent and try all kinds of options when it came to helping others. However, he had a deep inner understanding of when he needed to step away and he did not let the outside world influence his decision.

The willingness to walk away from situations that aren't right for you takes strength. It shouldn't come from a place of spite or meanness, but rather from valuing yourself and understanding the best use of your energy.

THE LESSON

There are certain situations and people that, for whatever reason, drain our energy or take us further away from ourselves. It's important to see the need to either temporarily or permanently take a break as needed.

THE PRACTICE

It's become commonplace to turn away from people we disagree with or who we think are "toxic" without doing the work of seeing what they trigger inside of us. Instead of dealing with ourselves and our own reactions to outside circumstances, we cut people out of our lives. This is different from understanding on a deep level when we need to withdraw our energy from situations that do not serve our greater good. Begin to really notice the situations in your life that leave you feeling drained of energy or emotionally uncomfortable. Next, sit quietly and ask what is needed from you in this instance. Is there something you need to learn from your own reaction? Or is it time to step out of the circumstance you find yourself in?

WHAT HELPS

Learning to value and trust yourself helps you to begin to understand the kind of life you want and the people you'd like to invite into it.

16.

HOUSEHOLD SPIRITS
ARE REAL THINGS

OVERALL IN THE United States, as far as I know, we don't have a strong collective experience that recognizes the fairies, brownies, or ancestors who watch over our homes. The folklore of many countries includes various kinds of creatures and spirits who help protect your home and even create a bit of mischief here and there. Most people have outgrown the idea that creatures like fairies and household spirits exist because we don't see them with our physical eyes.

Walter, on the other hand, actively worked with household guardians. Whenever I misplaced something in the house (which may or may not have happened regularly), Walter always told me to ask the household beings to help me find it. I have to tell you this always worked like a charm, even to the point where an item would show up someplace that I'd swear I had already looked multiple times!

One of Walter's most interesting encounters with fairies happened in Ireland. He was staying at a small, one-room cottage outside Dublin on a friend's property. The room he stayed in had floor-to-ceiling windows. He said he woke up one morning to some commotion outside his windows. He saw a group of fairies trying to get his attention, telling him to go and look at his front doorstep. When he opened the front door, he found a flower and a very small dead bird that had been carefully placed there. The fairies had left him these special gifts to welcome him to the cottage.

In every place I lived on the West Coast, the household spirits I saw looked a lot like what we think of as fairies or sprites. I was shocked to see an entirely different kind of household guardian when I moved to Colorado. I went online and found that what I was seeing closely aligned with images of brownies. I now suspect different parts of the country may attract different kinds of household spirits.

Household guardians are the ones to go to with specific asks about anything to do with your home or garden. They can help you find missing items, protect your home when you're away, alert you to issues within your house, and even inspire your creativity—especially about your home life. These little beings can often be seen out of the corner of your eye. In general, they are shy and like to stay hidden, but at the same time, they like it when you acknowledge them.

Yes, household guardians are real. Even if you don't think they are, why not take the opportunity, when you meditate or pray, to connect to the energy of your household? You can do a household health check, see if any issues—expected or unexpected—pop up, and give thanks for your home and all those who work toward its upkeep and care.

THE LESSON

Help comes to us in all different forms.

THE PRACTICE

Do you believe in magic? Sit in your home and see if you can sense your own household guardians while you meditate or pray. Have fun with this. Grab a journal and use your imagination to write down a conversation between you and your household guardians. If this idea is too "out there," you can also practice gratitude for your home and the shelter it provides. Make a list of all the things you appreciate about your home and give thanks for all of it.

WHAT HELPS

Let your mind be open and free. Find the sense of wonder and belief you had as a child.

17.

CONSISTENCY IS ONE OF
THE KEYS TO SUCCESS

Okay, the advice to be consistent may be one you've heard before from someone like Tony Robbins. Still, I want to share what I observed from watching a successful teacher, clairvoyant, and writer live his life. When it came to his work, Walter was incredibly consistent. Every day, every week, for over twenty years, he showed up. It didn't matter if he was talking to a room of five people or two hundred. If he planned a workshop or some other event, he put in the work and then carried it through. He did one-on-one work four days a week, classes just about every week, and Sunday services. He always offered his best to others.

This may be the first time you've ever heard of Walter. Many people knew him through his clairvoyant work and then later from *Spirit Babies*, the book he wrote. He wasn't a household name, but he was amazingly successful. His appointments were usually booked out three to four months in advance. He didn't advertise and almost all his work came from word of mouth.

It was amazing to watch someone put their best out into the world so consistently. I watched him do things that went well and were extremely successful. I was also there when something he tried fell flat and didn't work at all. Still, he always got back up and put himself out there over and over again.

Yes, many factors go into whatever we consider success. We absolutely do not live in a world with an even playing field for BIPOC and women. Still, I have seen firsthand someone with the inner discipline to be of service and to work with incredible dedication and consistency to achieve phenomenal goals. It left no doubt anywhere in me that, if there's something you want to succeed at, be consistent and keep trying. You may have to change what you're doing along the way, and you even may fail at times. Get back up, keeping going, and give the world the best you have to offer every day.

THE LESSON

Consistency is a powerful tool in our personal or professional lives. It's one of those things that's easy to talk about but hard to do.

THE PRACTICE

Establish small acts of faith in yourself. Pick a task and see if you can do it consistently for five days. Set yourself up to be successful by taking on something ridiculously easy. Notice what obstacles come up—because they will. Be ready for inner and outer resistance. Have a plan in place for what you will do when your consistency begins to slip and how you will regroup and start again.

WHAT HELPS

If consistency were easy, we'd all achieve it. Finding the inner discipline to be consistent can be a true challenge. Resistance is real. It is a force that exists all around us. Consistency asks us to master dancing with resistance—learning when to take a step forward and back but always sticking with the steps.

18.

EVERYTHING IS CONNECTED

WHEN WALTER AND I lived in Northern California, we would watch news stories about small earthquakes. Then a few days later, there'd be a report about an earthquake or volcanic activity someplace else in the world. The second report would always seem to end with the reporter stating the two events were not connected. Walter and I would shake our heads at each other because how can the Earth not be connected? We saw this happen constantly. We live in not just an interdependent universe, but also an interconnected one. Everything is connected—spiritually and energetically. We are one big ocean manifesting as individual waves.

One of the coolest things about this interconnectedness is understanding that you are already connected energetically to everything in this world. Spiritually, you don't lack anything because you are connected to all things. Everything you need, all the questions you want answered, are already part of you. The most basic definition of interconnectedness means to connect or to be or become mutually connected.

This aligns closely with interdependence, which means to be mutually reliant on each other. At the very least, we have come to understand more and more that we are an interdependent species. What happens in one part of the world does impact the rest. Solutions to problems discovered in one place can be applied across nations.

When we acknowledge the interconnectedness of the universe, we connect with a place of oneness that exists inside of us, a sense of harmony or what we may think of as being in the "zone" or flow of life. Some people experience this sense of flow as a feeling of abundance or prosperity. To me, it's that feeling of being in harmony with yourself and everything around you when your actions, emotions, or thoughts just seem to flow easily together.

As a clairvoyant, Walter had an impressive ability to work with energy. He understood and knew down in his bones that we are all connected. Now that doesn't mean we always get what we want when we want it. What he modeled for me over and over again, though, was his ability to open up to all the possibilities of life. He could get out of his own way and often energetically find what he needed, knowing he was already connected to it. Some people consider this the ability to manifest or pull the things you need into your life. You may also think of it as connecting the dots. If we're already connected to the information or thing we need, then it's just a matter of connecting the dots that will take us there.

Also, in an interconnected universe, you are never really alone. There may be times you feel lonely because that's part of being human. Spiritually and energetically, though, you are never alone. You are always connected to other people, spirit guides, and the higher energy force we think of as god, goddess, or creator. You are always a part of that larger energy, and it is part of you, expressing itself uniquely through you.

THE LESSON

In an interconnected universe, you are energetically connected to everything. There is no lack or scarcity from a spiritual point of view because you are connected to all things.

THE PRACTICE

You do not have to live in an either/or mental framework. We can be connected to all things, finding a flow and abundance within ourselves spiritually. At the same time, we can also acknowledge we live in an unjust world that requires our attention and action. We're quick to dismiss other people because we don't understand them, or they appear different. A concept like interconnectedness is easy to read about but much harder to embody. One small yet challenging action you can take is to truly attempt to understand someone else's point of view. Consider the circumstances that brought them to their beliefs. You don't have to agree with them or think they are right. Can you see their point of view, not agree with it, but also drop making them "less" and yourself "more" based on differing viewpoints? Imagine stepping into their shoes—and look out into the world.

WHAT HELPS

One way to support yourself in remembering that you are connected to everything is through meditation. Sit in any way that's comfortable for you so that you can breathe freely and deeply. Close your eyes and focus on the sound of your breath as it moves in and out of you. Place a hand in the middle of your chest over your heart chakra. Say either out loud or to yourself, "I am light, the light divine. All is light, the light divine." As you repeat this phrase let your body relax a little more with every exhale. Continue repeating this phrase as many times as feels right to you in the moment. When you feel the meditation is complete, open your eyes.

19.

PSYCHICS DON'T WANT TO READ YOU WHEN THEY AREN'T WORKING

I CAN'T TELL you the number of times people were uncomfortable being around Walter because he was a psychic, even though there were also definitely people who gravitated to him, intrigued by his experiences and wanting to know more.

But there were people very concerned about what he might see about them if they were around him in a social context. They worried he would learn all their secrets, all those things they didn't want anyone else to know about them. It was quite nerve-wracking for them to be around Walter.

Here's a little secret I did learn from him: psychics don't want to read you when they're not working. They may pick up an impression about you here and there, but truly, honestly, when they're off the clock, they aren't trying to see things about you.

There's a couple of reasons for this. First, when being a psychic is your job, the last thing you want to do is work when you have time off, just like anyone else. It's like how a doctor or therapist isn't trying to diagnose people when they are out socializing. Second, any ethical working psychic will not look into your business unless you specifically ask them to. It's like imagining an accountant would start telling you what they think about your finances during happy hour when you haven't asked. Same thing with psychics.

When a psychic isn't working, since they can't shut off their abilities, they shift their attention out of reading mode instead. So, if you find yourself hanging out with a psychic or clairvoyant, don't worry about what they're seeing about you because they aren't trying to get into your head and find out your deep, dark secrets. More than likely, they are experiencing you the same way non-clairvoyants do.

By the same token, if you happen to find yourself hanging out with a psychic, don't start asking them to look at your life, give you lucky numbers, ask who's going to win the next game, or when you'll meet your true love. They want to hang out, have fun, and not work too.

THE LESSON

Psychics are people too. They aren't out to secretly see whatever it is you don't want seen by a stranger.

THE PRACTICE

Let's expand the idea that there are things about us we may not want other people to see. Perhaps we feel these "hidden" parts would show a different side of us than the self-image we want to project in the world. This puts us in a precarious position—not just with psychics, but also anyone who gets close to us. All of us are human and we all have actions in our lives that we are not proud of or feel shame around. Begin the process of forgiving yourself by accepting that at any given moment, you are doing the best you know how.

WHAT HELPS

Each of us is a mix of what we consider "good" and "bad." When you can accept yourself for the wholeness of who you are, it won't matter what someone may see about you because you'll be comfortable with yourself.

20.

BEING PSYCHIC IS SOMETIMES THE PROBLEM

THERE'S AN OLD question, "Which came first, the chicken or the egg?" One of the things I learned from Walter is that people with psychic abilities sometimes create challenges in their lives by being psychic. Sound confusing? Let me digress into the Starfleet Prime Directive from *Star Trek*. It says members of Starfleet are not allowed to interfere with another culture or civilization. Well, when a psychic looks at a situation to see outcomes and dynamics, the very act of looking can interfere with what's going to happen. When Walter would look at future outcomes, he wouldn't just look at it one way. He would ask multiple questions from many different points of time and angles. It wasn't until I experienced this for myself that I understand what he was trying to avoid.

I had planned to attend a meditation retreat that was a couple of hours away from Denver. I had to hire a pet sitter to take care of, at the time, my really old dog and parrot.

After I made those arrangements, I kept getting a strong message that there was going to be a problem with the pet sitter. It kept coming from an intuitive voice that I always listen to when it speaks. I thought that taking a proactive step would take care of the issue. So I canceled my original pet sitter and hired someone else. The first day at the retreat I called to check in with the sitter and they said they were on the way to my house. Later in the day I tried and tried to reach them, but I couldn't get a hold of them. I called, texted, and emailed. No response. I'd been gone for over eight hours and I knew if my older dog had been left alone in the house, that wasn't a good thing. I had no other choice but to pack up my car and head home. I couldn't understand why the person hadn't shown up. I found out a couple of days later that they had been in a pretty bad car accident. That intuitive voice had been right; there had been a problem with the pet sitter. What I'll never know for sure is what would have happened if I had left the original pet sitter in place and accepted there might have been an issue. See the dilemma there?

Energy shifts, parallel universes, and different timelines all make it challenging for a psychic to see outcomes perfectly all the time. Sometimes when we try to make a certain outcome happen, we actually cause the problem we're trying to avoid.

THE LESSON

Sometimes, our task is to simply accept the moments of our lives as they present themselves instead of trying to change them.

THE PRACTICE

Of course, we want to change and control outcomes we consider unfavorable. What we are often unable to see or grasp is that a situation that appears unfavorable to our personalities may be in our lives for a bigger purpose or lesson. From ten feet away, what we perceive as something to be changed at 1000 feet is exactly what's needed to get us to the next place we need to be. We tend to pull ourselves away emotionally and physically from uncomfortable feelings and situations. When you experience a feeling that you don't "like," can you make the space and time to be quiet and sit with it? Can you hold a space for both the original feeling and the discomfort you feel with a sense of compassion and patience? See what happens if you stop pulling away and just feel.

WHAT HELPS

There is an ancient phrase attributed to the prophet Muhammed narrated by al-Tirmidhi that tells the story of a Bedouin man who was leaving his camel without tying it up. The Prophet asked why he did this, and the Bedouin replied that he put his trust in Allah. The Prophet said, "Tie your camel and place your trust in Allah." Another way of saying this is trust in God, and still secure your camel or take what action you can—but then trust and let go.

21.

WHEN YOU DECIDE TO MAKE A CHANGE, ALL THE REASONS NOT TO CHANGE WILL APPEAR

Look, I know there's the famous Goethe quote, "At the moment of commitment, the Universe conspires to assist you." I'm not disputing that quote. However, I will say that Walter always talked about how when we decide to change, anything holding us back or blocking us will come up. It's almost as if our resolve gets tested. So while the universe may conspire to assist you, it may also bring up your previous blocks so you can get past them.

The point Walter was making with this idea was twofold. First, when you decide to change, be prepared for things to pop up unexpectedly. Say you decide to start exercising in the morning before work. After a week or two, your car breaks down and you need to take the bus, so you need to leave earlier. Or the hours you work get changed, or maybe you have to move, and all your spare time is now dedicated to packing. Be ready for things to get in the way of your commitment and decide before you start how you'll handle those obstacles.

Second, setbacks are a normal part of change. For some people, it may feel like the universe is conspiring against them. It may feel like everything is getting in the way of the change or project before them. It's much more likely that our own patterns, fear and resistance are the culprits. Steven Pressfield wrote a brilliant book that's all about resistance, called *The War of Art: Break Through the Blocks and Win Your Inner Creative Battles*. It explores and acknowledges the major part resistance plays in our creative pursuits. Pressfield says, "We're wrong if we think we're the only ones struggling with Resistance. Everyone who has a body experiences Resistance."

As a common part of the change process, resistance comes in many forms. Let's go back to the idea of exercising in the morning. Say your car does break down and you do have to take the bus for a few days. Some people will let that throw them off track, others may take it as a sign from the universe that exercising in the morning isn't working. All sorts of other reasons to stop doing what you've decided to do will come up, and they may seem very logical and valid. However, they are also your resistance to making change and are there for you to see what you think is holding you back versus what actually is holding you back. If you pay attention, you might see that while on the surface your reason is something like you don't have the time, deeper within might be a fear of failure. Only you can decide if your dedication to change is worth dancing with resistance. If you do, you'll learn to keep knocking down those reasons or becoming very nimble working around them. What you won't do is give up on the change you want to make. You'll be ready to do battle with resistance and put strategies in place that keep you moving forward.

THE LESSON

When we commit to making a change or to a creative pursuit, all the reasons *not* to change will begin popping up.

THE PRACTICE

Understand that this is a normal part of change or any creative pursuit. Know that it's temporary and that you can move past it. Identify three blocks against the change you want to make, then think of three strategies per block that may help you get back on track as quickly as possible. Humor is also a great way to beat resistance. Be willing to shake your head and laugh at the obstacles you may face. It doesn't make them less challenging, but it helps to lighten and open our energy so that we can move past them as quickly as possible.

WHAT HELPS

There's nothing more frustrating than to decide you want to change only to have resistance suddenly pop up in an assortment of ways. Resistance, as Pressfield will you tell you, is sneaky. It comes in many forms. You try to change and yet things seem to be conspiring against you. Remind yourself that no one and nothing are overtly against you. It's merely resistance talking and distracting you from what you want to do. Laugh at it for being a trickster and then move on. Don't give it any more of your time and attention.

22.

WHO WILL YOU BLAME
WHEN I'M NOT HERE?

LONG BEFORE WE knew Walter had cancer, he would ask me, "Who will you blame when I'm not here?" He always asked this with equal amounts of seriousness and teasing. It would usually come up when I asked him to do something around the house. My joking reply was always, "You. I'll still blame you when you're not around."

This little exchange of ours brings attention to a dynamic that often appears in all kinds of relationships. We often subtly (or not so subtly) blame our inability to sustain a habit, make a change, or start something new on other people.

We can often feel imprisoned in our lives by other people's expectations and needs. We would take that dance class we've always wanted to take, but it happens during dinnertime. Our partners can't get dinner together; they're hopeless and the kids need to eat. There's just no way to make it to that class. If we do go, our partners will be mad that they had to make dinner, so it's just easier to forget the whole thing. Then we, consciously or unconsciously, blame our partners for holding us back. This thought process can unintentionally become a habit. We begin to accept there are things we could be doing with our lives if only this person or that didn't hold us back. Yet we might never have explained how important that dance class was to us. We might not have called the family together and said, "This is important to me. How can we work together to make it happen?"

Blaming other people for holding us back, or not supporting us enough, takes the responsibility for not making something happen off our shoulders. But the truth is, if our lives were suddenly to be cleared so that we could easily make a change or start something new, then we'd have to look at what part of us is actually holding us back. We think: If only I had the time, I could write that book or start exercising. However, when something is truly important to us, we will find a way to make it happen. It may take a while and it may not be perfect, but we make it happen.

Our ability to distinguish what might be holding us back from achieving something we want can get blurred in long-term relationships. We may think that if our lives and responsibilities were different, *then* we could do what we really wanted. When this kind of thinking rears its head, we have to stop and realize that we are the only ones who have the power to change our lives. We are the ones who must decide that something is important enough for us to change whatever patterns exist in our lives. We must realize we have had a hand in creating those patterns and responsibilities. Sometimes that means we've participated in creating certain behaviors in relationships by being passive, not speaking up, or going with the flow. The great news is we can also decide to change the terms of our relationships and life. It's not always easy and it can definitely create upheaval, but it's doable.

In the years since Walter died, I've gotten really clear about all the things I projected onto him. I've been able to look at all the expectations I had about him and our relationship. Projecting onto others is something we all do, and when a relationship ends, we get a chance to see more clearly what stuff was ours, what was theirs, and what was ours together.

THE LESSON

If we really want to change our lives in some way, big or small, we will find a way to do it. We may need to renegotiate how our relationships operate here and there, but we will make those efforts when it's important to us.

THE PRACTICE

It takes courage, awareness, and unwinding to see where we overtly or subtly blame others for the way things are in our lives. It is by no means easy to see how we have shaped our own lives when we've been blaming others. It can involve things like seeing how we don't stand up for ourselves or even how we ignore what other people tell us. Identifying the ways you blame other people for your circumstances is the first step. Then, instead of blaming, start looking for ways to make the changes that are important to you. Invite the people in your life to help and support you in making those changes. People who truly love you want you to succeed. If you keep a journal, you may want to add a weekly review of what you feel people in your life have "done" to you or what you feel is their "fault." Then write about your part in the situation.

WHAT HELPS

Remember it can be difficult to untangle our own inner world to see it clearly. It takes time and practice, so be patient with yourself.

23.

SOME PSYCHICS JUST TELL YOU WHAT YOU WANT TO HEAR

I WAS MARRIED to a very gifted clairvoyant. I'm not just saying that because he was my husband. If you talk to anyone he worked with, you'd hear the same thing. He was definitely the real deal. That being said, if you ever find yourself looking for an intuitive perspective, it's always good to get a referral from someone you trust. Like in any profession, some people are at the top of their game and others are not.

After Walter died, I set out to discover what other intuitives and psychics were like—how they operated or what type of information they offered. In doing so, I remembered that Walter once said, "There are readers out there who tell you want you to hear." They aren't doing it on purpose to fool you. When someone is first starting, they may be less skilled at reading energy. They see the energy of things you want around you and confuse that with where the energy is actually headed. Other times, a person offering you an intuitive perspective may be afraid to tell you something they think you won't like or won't want to hear. They are afraid of your emotional reaction. So instead, they try to come up with something they feel you'd want to hear. Again, this doesn't necessarily happen because a reader is being intentionally dishonest; it's more likely that they are still developing their skills.

It's so important when you work with a psychic, intuitive, or any kind of coach, that you only take in the information that resonates with you or is useful. You don't have to believe or use 100 percent of what someone offers you. Trust yourself and understand that even the most amazing advisor isn't going to be right all the time. Energy changes and shifts constantly. What was seen and shared in one moment could change an hour later because something shifted unexpectedly. All the spiritual and metaphysical divination systems and information out there are for us to understand ourselves and the world around us better, not necessarily to know the future.

Walter used to say we each had our own story that unfolded over a lifetime. Our individual stories have their own mythology and symbology. It's up to us to uncover, study, and learn the meaning of our own story with the tools we find along the way.

THE LESSON

As with any service profession, be choosy and careful. If something seems too good to be true, move forward with a certain amount of caution.

THE PRACTICE

There are times when we just want someone else either to tell us what to do or what's going to happen. Sometimes we do this against our own inner knowing or intuition. When you feel this way, the practice is to take a deep breath and sit with that feeling of wanting someone else to give answers to us. Deepen into it and see if you can feel or sense what is motivating you. See if you can acknowledge the emotions you find there like fear, worry, or confusion.

WHAT HELPS

Get a referral and trust yourself to know if something doesn't add up. Even if on the surface everything seems professional or "right", take a step back if your gut is telling you otherwise.

24.

KNOWLEDGE IS JUST KNOWLEDGE

No, saying "knowledge is just knowledge" isn't some anti-intellectual, anti-education rant. Walter was well on his way to getting his PhD when he changed course and became a full-time clairvoyant and spiritual teacher. The more spiritual work Walter did, though, the more he realized that knowledge isn't the answer to everything. In our society, we tend to collect knowledge, thinking the more we know, the more we will understand our lives. People can get into the habit of going to class after class and workshop after workshop, following the latest "thought leaders" to amass more and more knowledge. But have you noticed some of the people who go to every workshop and every big name lecture don't ever seem to change or actually apply that knowledge? We often think of knowledge as the ultimate power in our lives. If we just find that one piece of information we don't have, our lives will be different, transformed, and what we want them to be.

Everything has a place in this world. Knowledge serves

a purpose, especially within certain contexts. In the end, though, knowledge is just knowledge. It won't necessarily make you happy. It won't make you more aware. It's not the answer to enlightenment if that's your goal. Knowledge is a tool like many other tools in this world. Chasing more knowledge, accumulating more information on yet another path to self-knowledge or happiness, will not necessarily produce the change or understanding we seek. We can become so engrossed in knowing more that we get lost in stockpiling knowledge instead of implementing it.

Toward the end of his life, Walter strongly believed that the search for knowledge was more of a mental distraction than anything else. I think he felt focus, belief in yourself, and trust were all just as important as knowledge, yet we tend to value knowledge above each of these. It's not the answer to everything, especially when it comes to spirituality, self-understanding, and awareness.

THE LESSON

Don't go down the rabbit hole of stockpiling knowledge. Living your life, applying what you learn, and gaining experiences, are just as important. In the end, knowing more is not necessarily the answer to living your life.

THE PRACTICE

We place a high value on understanding and knowing things in our world. We may think we're learning and changing, but we may just be accumulating information. Are you a workshop junkie? Do you find yourself looking for the next shiny thing and deciding you must know about it? We all go through periods of acquiring information and learning. There's nothing wrong with that. However, think about whether you're doing more than acquiring knowledge. Are you applying it? Is it helping you? Is it useful to living your life or is it just more information? Go back to the last workshop or class you took. Did you use what you learned? If not, can you commit to applying the knowledge you've already acquired before you take another class or join another workshop?

WHAT HELPS

Notice what your relationship is to gathering knowledge. Are you searching for ultimate answers when it comes to living your life or your faith? Are you always looking for that next book or the teacher who's trending? These may be clues that you believe knowledge is the ultimate answer.

25.

MEET PEOPLE WHERE THEY ARE

As A SPIRITUAL teacher, Walter was extremely adept at meeting people where they were, not where he was. The best way I can illustrate this concept is to share a story about my Labrador Retriever puppy, Tucker. I had never lived with a Lab before Tucker. Many people warned me that they needed a lot of exercise to not be destructive. Armed with that knowledge, I proceeded to try to walk my six-month-old puppy—not for walks that were too long for his age, but still, I was determined to get him exercised. As a friend said, "I wanted to get his steps in." Now Tucker is an observer. He likes to sit and watch people, birds, squirrels, and other dogs go by. He didn't have a lot of use for me trying to "get his steps in." Here I was, bound and determined to tire him out, only to have him sit or lie down and refuse to move for a minute or two. I came away from these encounters frustrated and upset. After all, I was doing all this for him, right?

Finally, it dawned on me: this dog was not interested in walking up and down trails. He didn't want to walk the paved path around a pond. All this puppy really wanted was to go to a park with an open field and sniff around and meander. If another dog showed up who he could say hello to, even better. I hadn't been meeting Tucker where he was. I was meeting him where I thought he should be or where I was. We do the same thing with people. We put our expectations onto them, whether they are realistic or not, and wonder why they can't meet them. We talk to someone from our own point of view with no thought to where they are in a process or life. Then we scratch our heads and wonder why we're not connecting or why we're having trouble communicating.

Walter understood that to help people see their next steps, he needed to meet them where they were, not where he was, or where he thought they should be. He took the time to look at someone's situation from their point of view because that was the starting point that would be the most effective for him as a spiritual teacher.

THE LESSON

When we meet people where they are, it helps create a connection and a common starting point from which to move forward.

THE PRACTICE

We have a very difficult time stepping out of the shadow of our own all-consuming perspective. We have emotional and physical needs we want others to meet for us. Getting those met is often our priority, so we seldom really try to understand someone else's perspective. Can you take the time to consider how what you're doing may affect someone else? Can you let yourself imagine what it's like to stand in someone else's shoes and see what they might want or need? This is a good way to start the process of meeting someone where they are.

WHAT HELPS

Just like with Tucker, the Lab puppy, can you drop what you think or assume is needed and be present to what's happening in the moment? Awareness of what's presenting itself will help you meet others where they are. Also, simple exercises, like listening to the sound of your breath or noticing the feeling of your feet on the ground, can help you be more present and aware.

26.

IN A WORLD OF ILLUSION, WHY QUIBBLE ABOUT REALITY

THE NOTION OF the world is an illusion. Walter could see with absolute certainty the illusory form of what many of us think of as our normal, very real physical world. Like the nursery song, "Row, row, row your boat, gently down the stream / merrily, merrily, merrily, merrily life is but a dream," Walter saw, felt, and knew this world was a temporary dream. Therefore, he'd say why quibble about reality? He and I used to joke that we should get T-shirts printed with some form of this quote because it was so important to remind ourselves of it.

For me, this quote can go in many different directions, but much of it has to do with being "right" about something or thinking there are "absolutes" in this life. For instance, some religions may believe their way is the only way. However, in a world that's more like a hologram a la the move *The Matrix*, what is reality, anyway? If this life is a temporary dream, an illusion, or hologram that merely feels real, is there really any one absolute we must insist on? There is a Sufi proverb that says, "There are as many paths to God as there are souls on Earth." I would add there are as many different realities as there are souls on Earth, too. Each of us experiences this world from our unique perspective. Two people in the exact same situation, at the exact same time, will not have the same experience. Their reactions, what they take in, and how they process the experience will all be different. It's the same shared moment, yet in many cases, two completely different realities.

I think about a disagreement I had with a friend over a previous conversation we had. I came away from it very angry. I felt like my friend had been completely insensitive to what was going on in my life, even condescending. When we came back together to try to reconcile what had happened, we had two very different perspectives. They insisted they had been trying to be helpful, that their goal was to be supportive. Quite frankly, I was gob smacked by this because I truly don't know in what reality that was the case. Still, this was an instance where we both wanted to move on, we were both sorry for the rift, and we could both see there was no point in insisting our perspective was the real, *right* one. In the end, we both understood it wasn't good for our friendship to quibble about reality and we moved on.

So much conflict seems to arise out of one philosophy— whether it be religious, political, or even personal—vying for the top spot, for dominance. We get so mired in the weeds that we forget to balance that with the finite, temporary nature of this reality.

THE LESSON

There are as many different realities as there are people.

THE PRACTICE

Bring awareness to those moments where you find yourself insisting *your* perspective or reality is the right, true one. Sit with the idea that more than one reality can exist side by side. Take a step and look at what's important in the moment. Of course, there will be times when, for whatever reason, you must stick with your position. But there will probably be even more times when you need to remind yourself that in a world of illusion, why quibble about reality?

WHAT HELPS

Let go of wanting to be right, of insisting the only reality that's right is yours. Of course, also be aware that if someone else's "reality" invites harm to others, that requires action and not passivity.

27.

OUR SPIRITUAL LIVES UNFOLD
IN SACRED, NOT LINEAR TIME

YOU KNOW THAT saying, "People make plans and God laughs"? The idea of sacred time versus linear time is similar. Sacred time is an idea Walter talked about often. It transcends the idea of this physical world, crossing dimensions and our concept of time and lifetimes.

In these human bodies, we think of time as linear, and we generally expect our lives to be as well. However, our concept of time is really a shared illusion. One of Walter's favorite illustrations about this was daylight saving time. Twice a year in the United States, most of us agree time moves forward or backward an hour. Boom! Just like that, the country completely changes our agreement and belief about time.

Our spiritual journey or self-development unfolds in sacred time. It may not make sense to us, nor can we understand why it can't happen faster, sooner, or differently. We can be impatient when working with spiritual concepts, or we may not understand why our lives have taken a certain turn. Walter taught that sacred time has its own pace. He usually said this when I was impatiently complaining about why something I wanted to happen wasn't happening. I understand now that what he meant was the patterns and circumstances of our lives unfold in their own way, on their own timetable, and definitely not in a way we can hurry or control. If life is like a stream, sometimes the stream moves fast and sometimes slow—irrespective of the speed we may want it to go at any given moment.

There is a mystery to our lives and spiritual selves that asks us to cultivate acceptance and trust. Trust is a big one. We must trust ourselves to find the teachings or teachers that resonate with our journey. We must trust ourselves to take leaps of faith as needed. We must trust our trajectory, knowing we won't miss anything and that our spirit is always guiding us. Our spiritual lives and understanding unfold in sacred time. It may not be on our schedule, but as Shakespeare's Hamlet said, "There are more things in Heaven and Earth, Horatio, than are dreamt of in your philosophy."

THE LESSON

Our spiritual lives are not governed by linear time. Whatever spiritual beliefs you live by, whatever teachings you follow, they will work their way through your life in sacred time.

THE PRACTICE

When our lives don't seem to take the path we want, we can feel impatient and angry. The best way to work with this is acceptance, acceptance, and acceptance. Let yourself trust that on a spiritual level, everything is always on track and operates outside of linear time. Meditation can be a very helpful way to embrace the acceptance of what is happening in your life in this moment.

WHAT HELPS

Our physical world is heavily governed by linear time. We want things to have a start and an end. We don't want to be late; we want to be on time; we want to do things on a schedule. Try to remind yourself that our spiritual lives just don't work that way. Know there is a bigger plan unfolding in your life. In every moment, you are exactly where you need to be.

28

NEVER MAKE RESOLUTIONS IN JANUARY

THE ADVICE NOT to make resolutions in January is a funny one considering Walter also said, "Everything works some of the time." It seems like in recent years, at least in the United States, we've started to move away from making New Years' resolutions and have taken up practices and intentions instead. Really, whenever you decide to make a change and can stick to it is a good time to do it. Still, let me share why January isn't the best time energetically to make changes to your life. By the way, this is for those who live in the northern hemisphere, and particularly North America, where it's winter in January.

First, the holiday season for many people ends on January 1. That means people have just been through a series of fall and winter holidays that may have been stressful, busy, and energy depleting. On top of that, the energy coming from the Earth is at a low point. There's less light during the day and it's not a time of growth. Most plants and many animals have gone into hibernation mode. So, at a time many of us want to turn inward and huddle next to the fireplace, our society says it's a new year, make changes.

In comparison, think about springtime, especially late spring. It stays light outside for longer and nature begins to green up and grow again. We feel a sense of buoyancy and renewal the closer we get to the end of spring and beginning of summer. The energy at this time of year naturally gets us active again. In general, we feel more supported by the energy of the Earth at this time.

In the dead of winter, after the whirlwind of the holidays, just say no to resolutions. Instead, lie low or gently get back into the rhythm of post-holiday life. If you need to have a regular time of year to make resolutions or change, consider late spring and get in step with the energy of the seasons.

THE LESSON

Do what works for you. Don't buy into arbitrary cultural customs or celebrations unless you find them useful.

THE PRACTICE

Instead of making resolutions or intentions in January, let yourself dream about the spring. What new seeds do you want to plant in your life during springtime? Dream big, but also think about what smaller, concrete steps will help you make your intention a reality.

WHAT HELPS

Life can feel easier when we go with the flow. Still, it's important to figure out what works best for you. Just because everyone else is doing it doesn't mean you have to. Your mom might have been right on that one.

29.

WHEN YOU'RE SUCCESSFUL, EVERYONE WANTS TO KNOW YOUR STORY

OKAY, I'LL ADMIT there were many times when I was younger that I aspired to a certain kind of fame and notoriety. At any given time, that could mean being someone who had a best-selling book or was a well-known speaker. I would fall into the comparison game and wonder why other people achieved what I wanted while I felt so far away from where I wanted to be. I would look at other women who seemed to have vast networks of close and social friends and wonder why that wasn't part of my life. I compared myself to people I had no business comparing myself to, and in doing so, I caused myself unnecessary suffering. I was also not focused on the real work.

One day, when I'm sure I was (annoyingly) lamenting something along these lines to Walter, he said something to me I'll never forget: "Stop worrying about what everyone else is doing or what you think you don't have." He went on to say, "Focus on the work you want to do and stop worrying about what you'll get out of it. I can guarantee that when someone is successful, everyone wants to know their story."

I think this was his sneaky way of redirecting my focus back on *doing* the work instead of the daydreaming about what I wanted to get out of it. At that point in my life, I'd wanted to be noticed, affirmed, and liked by others. He was reminding me that when I focus and act on the work I want to do, momentum happens.

Today, what I want out of life has changed considerably from when Walter said, "When you're successful, everyone wants to know your story." I'm sure he only said that to me once, but it's one of those things that will stay with me forever. It's a simple statement with multiple lessons in it for me. It's a solid reminder that whatever work you're doing, when done well, will attract people into your sphere. When we see someone who is focused on their work, giving it their best effort, and feeling excited and successful in their own accomplishments, aren't we interested to hear more about that person?

The bottom-line message was:

- Stop comparing yourself to other people
- Stay in your lane
- Do the work in front of you
- Find your own standard of success

This was typical of Walter. He could break things down in a way that got you to focus on what's essential and to change your thinking to something more effective and expansive.

THE LESSON

The three biggest takeaways are it's never too late to do what you want to do; don't compare yourself to others; and do the work in front of you.

THE PRACTICE

The first step is to begin to notice when you compare yourself to others. Once you notice you've started the compare game ask yourself what success means to you. Remember that despite what it looks like on the surface you really don't know what someone else's life is really like. Look at the difference between being good at what you do versus your expectations and yearnings for what you want in your life. Are you hoping your work will deliver those expectations and yearnings to you? Is that realistic? Remind yourself there's only one you in this world. What you have to offer is unique because you're the one doing it.

WHAT HELPS

We all have dreams about what an amazing amount of success would look in like our lives. We may dream of big houses and expensive cars, or knowing other leaders in our field. We compare ourselves to other people, looking at what we think they have that we don't. Comparison leads to creating our own world of suffering because we only see what we think is lacking in our lives. When you find yourself comparing your life to someone else's, stop and turn the focus back on your work and your journey.

30.

THERE'S MORE TO KARMA
THAN YOU MAY THINK

YOU MAY HAVE heard sayings like, "Karma is a bitch," or when someone does something we don't consider nice, "Their karma will take care of that." People think karma is only this straight "cause and effect" that both punishes and rewards our actions: "I did something mean and the universe will send meanness back to me." This has always confused me because I've seen the unkindest, most self-absorbed people be incredibly successful in life. In fact, they seem to be rewarded for doing what will get them what they want no matter who's hurt in the process. I've heard people explain this by saying, "Well, if not in this life they will get what's coming to them in the next life."

On this planet, we certainly live under the law of cause and effect. Whether that's karma, I'm not sure. Walter had a very different explanation about karma, and it makes a lot of sense to me. Here's the story he used to tell. Imagine you grew up in a family where your great-grandfather, grandfather, and father were lawyers. Each generation that came along was expected to be lawyers and work in the family business. Your siblings are lawyers and even your cousins are too. Your whole life, all anyone in your family has done is given you the option of being a lawyer, so much so that it never occurs to you to not be one. It's like you're wearing blinders; and even though there are a million other careers out there you might enjoy and that you might be really good at, all you can see is being a lawyer.

Karma is the patterns or grooves in our lives that are so ingrained in us that we don't see any other possibilities. It doesn't even occur to us that there is a world beyond these patterns. In essence, we are asleep to anything but what this programming automatically follows.

Working with a spiritual or self-awareness practice can help us become aware of those patterns and grooves, because they all manifest differently for each of us. Can we wake up and see the bigger picture? Awareness doesn't mean you don't choose to be a lawyer. It means you allow yourself to see all your options so you are deciding from an expanded and awakened point of view rather than an unconscious, automatic one.

THE LESSON

When it comes to seeing ourselves clearly, we all have unseen areas. It's often the very patterns that we can't see without digging into some self-work that affect our lives the most.

THE PRACTICE

Karmic patterns can be especially difficult to see on your own because they run deep and often through our family lineage. You may consider keeping a daily journal and noting the things in your life that are difficult or make you feel uncomfortable. Sometimes, it's something as simple as your neighbor leaving their garbage can out all week and it's driving you crazy. Over a few months, can you look back at your notes and sense a theme or recurring pattern? This will give you insight into what to focus on in your self-development work.

WHAT HELPS

Getting help from someone a little farther down the path when it comes to looking at the patterns that keep us caged and that we feel are impossible to change is important. Finding guidance that helps you develop awareness about yourself and expand your viewpoint is a key step in self-development. When you're frustrated with yourself or feel like you can't make the changes you want, remember help is out there. Go and get it!

31.

AS LONG AS YOU'RE ALIVE, YOUR STORY ISN'T OVER— ANYTHING IS POSSIBLE

SOMETIMES, I'D SAY to Walter that I wished my life were this way or that way. Maybe I'd dreamed of having a group of women friends like on *Sex and the City* or *Steel Magnolias*. Another day, maybe I wished I were a successful author. Often, when I would wish aloud for something, he'd reply with something like, "As long as you're alive, your story isn't over." There's always more to do and to be revealed. It's funny how in every decade of our lives, there's some part of us that thinks it's "too late" and we've somehow missed the boat. That's all in our heads. It's only too late if we put that limitation on ourselves.

His point was a simple one. As humans, we can get stuck in our own stories and feel like nothing will ever change for us. There are moments when we can't imagine our lives expanding beyond our current situation. Walter firmly believed that as long as one lives, anything can happen. This perspective came from his belief in how humans are built to function energetically. When the divine heart (also called the fourth chakra) is open, it gives us hope and allows us to see all the possibilities that can exist and occur in our lives.

No matter how desperate a situation seems, the heart chakra insists that there's always a possibility for change. An open heart lets us access the largest arena of choice and possibility that exists to create a life of inspiration and hope. The constant message of an open fourth chakra is that everything is possible.

When we dream about what we want out of life—a home, financial success, a family—we are pulling a stream of possibilities out of the heart chakra. The possibilities that exist for us never go away. At any point in our lives, all the millions of possible outcomes exist all at once, waiting for us. More often than not, it's our own inability to step away from the stories of "I can't," "I don't deserve it," "It's someone else's fault," "This is always how it goes for me," and whatever other stories we tell ourselves that keep us from experiencing the different possibilities that exist.

Our time here on Earth is finite. We only get so much time and then the person we are is gone. There are difficult times when our days feel endless, but really, our lives come and go more quickly than we think. As long as you are still here, as long as you can let yourself move past your stories of lack and limitation, tremendous possibilities exist for you. Your life story isn't over. What do you want the next moment, the next day, the next week, month, and year to look like? Move past the patterns that keep you stuck and find the possibilities that exist all around you in every moment.

THE LESSON

We often feel our lives are set in a certain direction or trajectory and there's no hope for change. As long as you're alive, there is always the possibility for something different, for change, for something more.

THE PRACTICE

New possibilities don't mean no conflicts or difficulties. New possibilities sometimes require us to be brave and to have faith in ourselves. Sometimes, we have to dream a bigger dream for ourselves than we can imagine. Our minds and thoughts can keep us stuck as they throw out problems and negativity. We often try to think everything out before anything has actually happened. At times, we need to get out of our heads and reconnect with our emotions and body. Don't let any negative or defeatist thinking stop you from opening to new things. Instead, put on music and dance, or get out in nature and walk around. Sit by the ocean or a stream or lake and watch the water go by. Get out of your head and out of your own way.

WHAT HELPS

The truth is we are often the only person standing between us and the possibilities of our life. How we think and the stories we tell ourselves all play a role in limiting our ability to access the possibilities that exist in every moment. As long as you're alive, your story isn't over, anything is possible. Change your thinking, change your life.

32.

LIFE ONLY HAS THE MEANING YOU GIVE IT

WE GROW UP with values and morality instilled in us, the content varying widely depending on the belief system our parents and caretakers followed and passed on to us. As a society, we decide what meaning and value we assign to the pieces of our world. We mostly accept these meanings unconsciously.

However, as co-creators of our universe, we are actually the ones who assign value and moral judgment to our actions. An example of this is how our collective societal norms change over time. In general, our attitudes towards women's equality, LGTBQ+, and human rights have changed over time. In the same way, we judge how we think our lives are going based on the value we assign to certain outcomes. We like this; we don't like that. But much of what we react to or judge about ourselves and our lives comes down to our subjective perception about a situation and how we choose to value and frame it.

For example, what if you tried seeing failure as a positive force in your life? Instead of it making you depressed or feeling like a loser, think of each failure as bringing you one step closer to where you need to be. What if you looked at the people you clash with not just as irritating, but rather as reminders for you to cultivate patience when you're annoyed with yourself and others?

Our minds and thoughts absolutely have the power to shape not just our inner world, but also how we perceive the outside world. For instance, there may be help all around you, but you can't see it because our society's values say strong, independent people don't need help. So no matter how much help is around you, it won't even register.

One of Walter's superpowers was being like the character Neo from the movie *The Matrix*. Behind both the beauty and the ordinary parts of this world, he understood that good and bad are two sides of the same coin. Like in *The Matrix*, they are just a stream of 0s and 1s that we run with to create reality, depending on our particular programming.

THE LESSON

When you're able to see your part in co-creating your life's value and meaning, you can also start to see ways to expand and change.

THE PRACTICE

This is not an easy practice. You must have a true desire to see past your own "programming" because, like in *The Matrix*, our reality feels extremely real, defined, and set. If you want to change your life a good place to start is by changing the way you think *about* your life. One way to do this is by simply noticing where your attention is when something bothers you. Is it in the past reliving something that is over, is it in the future projecting what *could* happen, or is it in the present?

WHAT HELPS

Being open to questioning your beliefs about the world and who you are is important. We see how other people can create their own problems or hardships because they refuse to see there might be another path. We *all* do that. So be open to seeing outside the box you've put yourself in.

33.

PSYCHICS HAVE A HARD TIME SEEING THEIR OWN FUTURE CLEARLY

SEEING OURSELVES AND our journeys clearly can be challenging. We are attached to our own well-being and the loved ones around us. After Walter, a non-smoker, not suddenly but nevertheless unexpectedly died of stage IV lung cancer, I had someone say to me, "Well, he must not have been much of a psychic if he didn't see that coming." Obviously, this person didn't know Walter, so they hadn't experienced what an amazingly talented clairvoyant he truly was. Still, we all have parts of ourselves that are impossible to see, or we aren't necessarily meant to see. Walter was attached to me, his dogs, parrots, and his work. While his soul came to the end of its journey on this plane, there was a part of Walter that was attached to staying. So, it's not surprising to me that he didn't see his own death coming clearly. In fact, he was a warrior, fighting the cancer and trying to stick around as long as possible.

While Walter could see many, many things about our lives clearly, the deaths of any loved ones were always murky for him. We had a series of pets over our time together. I was always the one who made decisions about when it was time to let them go. That was something he just couldn't do.

Intuition and clairvoyance don't make someone infallible. A psychic is, after all, an ordinary person who has honed these skills. Just like the rest of us, they lack clarity about certain parts of themselves and their future.

THE LESSON
Psychics are people too.

THE PRACTICE
The people in our lives can be very talented in their profession except when it comes to their own lives. Can you become aware of your expectations about the people in your life you consider experts? Is there anyone in your life who you feel "should" have answers for you? We often elevate people who we respect and feel have something to teach us instead of realizing they are fellow travelers. Look at how you view the dynamics of these relationships, including the balance of power and responsibility.

WHAT HELPS

Remember we all have limited vision when it comes to seeing ourselves clearly—full stop. One of the reasons we work with others when it comes to our personal development is because we need the mirror they provide. We can't see every aspect of ourselves clearly, it's just not possible.

34.

IF YOU HAVE A BODY, YOU STILL HAVE KARMA

OKAY. DEPENDING ON what circles you run in, you may or may not encounter people who say things about having no unfinished business or karma in this life. One of my favorite "Walterisms" is his response to people who would make this kind of claim. I so clearly remember him saying this more than once during one of his Sunday services. He'd thump his fist on his chest and say, "If you want to know if you still have karma in this life, look down. If you're in a body, you still have karma." I don't know why, but this always cracked me up.

You may be thinking, "What does this have to do with me? I'm not into karma." Fair enough, but at some point in your life, you may think it's too late for you to do something. Or you may get weary of your life and feel like there isn't much more here in this world for you to discover. That's when remembering this will come in handy. If you're still alive, then there *are* still things for you to explore and it's not too late.

When you get to those moments when you feel like you're finished or you've done everything you wanted to accomplish, it's time for a new perspective. As long as you're still in a body, there's more to learn, practice, and explore. When one journey ends, another one can begin. If you've cultivated some awareness about yourself and your life, then you get to choose which new journey to start. There's a reason you're here even when feelings of boredom, sadness, or depression may try to tell you differently.

If your life feels a bit stale and like you've come to a dead end, the good news is you can change that. When we take charge of the stories we tell ourselves, we can set a new course for our lives. Letting go of the narratives that no longer serve us is part of realizing there's still more of life for us to explore. Can you stop looking at life as something "to do", and instead look at it as something to experience?

THE LESSON

Look down. If you have a body, you're alive and there's more to explore.

THE PRACTICE

We can get into grooves and slumps that sometimes make us feel like there's no point in continuing or we're done with our lives the way they are. Alternatively, our egos may tell us we no longer have any karma in this world. When this happens it's time to shake up your life and try something new.

Do things that spark your interest. Take a weekend road trip and experience someplace different. Go and sit completely still out in nature and notice everything around you. Stop thinking about your own situation and go volunteer and do good for others.

WHAT HELPS

Sometimes, we get tunnel vision and don't clearly see the enormous world outside that tunnel. Our whole reality can become full of unhelpful thoughts and feelings. One of the best ways to get out of your head when this happens is to do something physical. Get your body moving and take a walk, ride a bike, or dance around your house.

35.

IF YOU'RE HONEST, YOU DON'T HAVE TO BROADCAST IT

I HAVE VIVID memories of driving around town with Walter. Whenever we'd pass by a business with the word "honest" in it, like Honest Auto Repair, he always commented on it. "Nope," he'd say, "if they have to say they're honest, they're not." I thought this commentary was both funny and interesting. After all, maybe honesty was so important to a business owner that they made it part of their business name. I think I must have even said something like this to him at some point. I remember him telling me to always pay careful attention to people who felt the need to assert that they were honest, kind, superior…whatever. He explained that in his experience, people who felt the need to broadcast a certain attribute, like honesty, seldom were.

Here's the thinking behind this. People or businesses that are honest don't give it a second thought. They don't have to; it's just part of who they are and how they operate. It never occurs to them that they need to tell other people they are honest. It goes without saying. And as they interact with others, people understand that from working with them. People who aren't honest do feel the need to broadcast it because they think saying it makes it seem like they are or will make it so.

Okay, don't freak out and get all up in arms if you feel like this may apply to you. Just think about it. This is one of those pearls of wisdom you need to check out for yourself. Your life is one grand experiential testing ground. Look around and start paying attention to people who feel the need to broadcast their attributes. See what you think. Is this a true thing or not? By the way, this also applies to anyone who goes around bragging about how good they are at doing anything. If they have to brag about their skills all the time to anyone who will listen, be skeptical. Just saying.

THE LESSON

Actions speak louder than words. Your words should always reflect your actions, not the other way around.

THE PRACTICE

Let yourself notice how people and businesses position themselves versus the reality of your experience. Can you see the disconnect when people tell you one thing, but then do something completely different? We have almost all had the experience of looking at a situation in hindsight and thinking "I knew I shouldn't have done that"—and yet we did. Do you have an unconscious bias in place, such as, "Well, they're a professional, so I thought I should believe them?"

Or "But they seemed to understand me?" We all have biases that make us more likely to believe someone, even when our intuition is trying to get our attention. Be mindful of who you believe and why. You don't have to change it or judge it; just start with seeing what's there.

WHAT HELPS

Trust your intuition. If you get a weird sensation or a vibe that tells you something is not aligning in an interaction, make a note of it so you can keep track of your feelings and the outcome.

36.

DON'T TAKE IT PERSONALLY BECAUSE MOST PEOPLE AREN'T THINKING ABOUT YOU

NOT TAKING THINGS personally is a classic Walter nugget of wisdom. He always knew his audience. I used to take things extremely personally when we first met. I think many of us do, and I still struggle with this lesson at times. Whether it's the driver who cuts you off or the co-worker who somehow forgets to include you when they ask everyone else to lunch, it's not about you. Yet somehow, we take it very personally. "How could they do this to me?" we ask ourselves. Mostly, people are thinking about themselves, not you. They are looking at what's in front of them. It's not just you they aren't thinking about, it's everyone else too, period. Yes, of course, there are times when someone is directing something at you specifically, but my guess is 98 percent of the time, no one else is thinking about you.

This ties into something Brené Brown talks about—"the

stories we tell ourselves." It's the stories we make up about why people are doing something we perceive as being done "to us" without ever knowing what the other person is actually thinking. We personalize other people's actions. Usually, it's when something we are insecure about gets triggered. It may be something we haven't dealt with or processed that has nothing to do with the current situation, yet we project a story about it onto the people around us. We personalize it. And while we're personalizing their actions, they're doing the same thing to us.

When someone tells us not to take something personally, it can feel demeaning and even offensive, as if they are saying our feelings don't matter. However, people's actions and behavior tell us far more about themselves than us. This doesn't mean we don't get hurt or angry when people treat us badly or unfairly. However, when we get wrapped up in what someone's done to us, we also rent out space in our heads to them. Energetically, we either tie ourselves to them through our outer emotional reactions, or our inward processing, trying to figure out what we did wrong.

This isn't to say nothing is ever our responsibility and everyone else is the problem. However, it does give us a starting point for clarity in sorting out our interactions with other people. On any given day, whether we're in line at the grocery store or putting gas in our car, we can find ourselves taking total strangers' actions personally. A good example of this happened to me while I was standing in line at Whole Foods. The person in front of me was taking an exceedingly long time to check out. They were chatting with the clerk and then halfway through the transaction, decided to rush over and buy a plant.

I found myself getting increasingly angry that neither this person nor the cashier seemed to have any regard for my time. Then once it was my turn, as the cashier was checking me out, this same customer took my cart back outside to where all the other carts were before I realized what was happening. Let me tell you I was so angry that day I immediately started to wonder what the hell was wrong with that woman and why she was treating me this way. I fumed all the way back to my car. As I sat in my car, getting angrier by the minute, I suddenly stopped and remembered not to take it personally because she wasn't even thinking about me. As soon as that realization entered my mind, I started to laugh. I saw how quickly my mind made up a story and took the whole interaction to heart. That woman was in her own world that had nothing to do with me. It wasn't personal. I just happened to be there when she was. Did I experience a petty inconvenience that took more of my time than I would have liked? Yep, but that was all it was. I quickly shifted my thinking and became more interested in what had prompted such an intense reaction in me, what caused me to take it so personally, instead of focusing on what she "did to me."

Start by assuming people aren't purposely doing something "to you" that's mean or negative in some way. Assume they aren't trying to hurt or offend you intentionally. Don't personalize it until you actually know whether the story you're telling yourself is true. Don't take it personally because most of the time, people aren't thinking about you.

THE LESSON

Don't take things personally when you don't know what's truly going on. Don't think, without any conversation or confirmation, something's about you. Most people are busy trying to navigate their own lives and aren't thinking about your point of view.

THE PRACTICE

It takes a lot of bravery not to take things personally. We have to be brave enough to look at ourselves and understand our insecurities and the things that set us off. We also have to be brave enough to communicate with other people instead of taking something personally. We have to be willing to feel vulnerable and ask someone what they meant or what they intended. Initiating a conversation like that can feel very scary. Be brave.

WHAT HELPS

Relationships can be an amazing source of connection for us. They can also make us crazy at times because through them, we bump up against our own stuff. Managing our inner life, including our projections and the stories we tell ourselves, can be a delicate balance. Let yourself think of the opportunity to practice not taking things personally as a gift to yourself.

37.

WE LIKE TO HAVE FRIENDS WHO VALIDATE OUR COMPLAINTS

WE DON'T NECESSARILY think about the nature of our friendships until someone points this out. Once they do, though, it's wild how true it is. Think about your friends. Now think about the different situations that come up in your life. The circumstances that annoy, offend, or hurt you, or you just don't understand. Now think about who you would call first in those moments. Most of the time, you'll find yourself reaching out to the friend who you know will "get it," or, in reality, who will agree with your assessment or complaint. On the other hand, there's the friend you would definitely not call regarding certain situations. Mainly because on some level, you know they won't agree with you.

This is human nature. It's not good or bad, but what's interesting to look at is which friends you turn to for what. Also, maybe instead of reaching out to the friend who will validate your complaint, consider calling the friend who absolutely won't. What would happen if you did that? Yeah, you might get irritated and not feel heard. But maybe it would be good to get a different perspective—to actually be *open* to a different perspective. Having your perspective validated can sometimes create an impasse or stoke the flames. Being open to a friend with a different perspective can help you let go of a situation and move on to a more useful solution or a more measured emotional response.

This can be tricky to do, especially when you're already upset or frustrated. You can easily turn that frustration onto the friend who doesn't validate your complaint, and that's not good for anyone. If you're going to do this, it must be done with the awareness that you've decided to take a different path and try something unusual. It's an exercise in awareness to see a different perspective and to look at what your expectations are around friendship. It's an opportunity to look at why you feel you need someone else to validate your complaint or make you feel right in the situation you're analyzing. Again, it's not good or bad to feel that way, but it's an excellent opportunity to look at your friendships and see if what holds some of them together is being able to complain to each other—or rather, something more positive.

THE LESSON

Be aware of whether you curate your friendships based on their willingness to agree with you or say you're in the "right" depending on the situation.

THE PRACTICE

Bringing awareness to why we turn to certain friends when we want validation is a great mindfulness practice. A good exercise may be talking to a friend who you know *won't* validate your complaints. Instead, they can provide a different perspective and help you reframe and change the energy—rather than stoke it. You may also want to ask yourself if you are actually looking for support or if you want to be right.

WHAT HELPS

We all want to feel heard and acknowledged by our friends. Becoming aware of which friends you turn to when you want a particular response can be challenging, especially if being right is important to you. We all need emotional support, but consider learning to receive it from friends without needing them to agree with your point of view or validate your complaints about a situation.

38.

DON'T APPOINT YOURSELF AS SOMEONE'S TEACHER WHEN THEY HAVEN'T ASKED FOR ONE

IN ADDITION TO being a clairvoyant, Walter also channeled two specific spirit guides. I was probably in my early thirties when I was talking to one of these guides about my mom. My mother was a complicated person and being one of her children came with its own challenges. I asked this guide about confronting my mother over things that had gone on while I was a teenager. The guide asked me point blank if I wanted to take on the role of teacher for my mom, and that stopped me in my tracks. Heck no, I didn't want to do that! The guide explained to me that when we want to make someone see something or acknowledge something they haven't asked us about, we are in essence appointing ourselves as their teacher. I could have confronted my mom, but I doubt she would have seen or acknowledged what I "felt" she should. In fact, I know it would have ended in a big blowup.

This idea really struck home with me. There will always be instances when we interact with someone and think things like, "Do they realize that… ?" or "I wonder if I should be the one to point out…?" Whenever I hear myself thinking along those lines, I ask myself, "Did this person ask you to be their teacher?" The answer is always no, they did not.

This doesn't mean we don't learn from other people, because of course we do. This idea specifically refers to that moment when *we* decide it's time for someone else to "learn" about something or have something pointed out unprompted. This is our desire to make someone see something they may not be ready to see. Once I started to think about these instances in terms of appointing myself, unasked, as someone's teacher, it changed how I approached others.

Just to be clear, I'm not talking about instances when we are out in the world and someone is harassing another person because of their sex, skin color, religion, sexuality, etc. That's something different. In those situations, we must stand up to hate and negativity.

THE LESSON

It can be easy to think we should tell people about themselves. Maybe we want to do this out of love or because we want to "help" the other person. You must decide if you want to appoint yourself as someone's teacher when they haven't asked for one.

THE PRACTICE

It's so much easier to see someone else's challenges and blocks than it is to see our own. It can also be that we feel justified in pointing these things out to someone else because we don't like what they are doing or how they are living. Still, appointing ourselves as someone else's teacher often creates more problems than it solves. Can you notice when you feel the urge to give unsolicited advice or point out something to others? Notice who you feel the urge to "educate", or if it's always when certain topics come up. When someone is confiding in you, take the time to ask if they need to vent or if they are looking for ideas/solutions. Lastly, when you want to volunteer unsolicited advice, wait for a day or two and see if you still feel it's needed.

WHAT HELPS

Honoring the path that someone else is on is a big one. They will see something about themselves or their situation when they are ready. If they come to you and specifically ask for your help, that's one thing. If you decide it's your place to give opinions on someone else's life and choices, that's usually not appreciated. Of course, parents are an exception to this because they are our first teachers in all things human.

39.

SOMETIMES IT'S THE LESS DIRECT ROUTE THAT GETS YOU WHERE YOU NEED TO GO

I HAVE NO context for the memory. Nevertheless, I remember noticing Walter was rubbing my elbow one day. Now one may think, "How lovely! What a sweet and loving gesture." Yes… but I knew my husband well. I looked at him and said, "You're doing some kind of energy work on me, aren't you?" He cracked up. "Yep, the elbow is a less direct way into your heart chakra. I'm trying to move some blocks. If I tried to do it directly, your defenses would go up. This way is less direct, but it lets me get in there to do some work."

It's funny how certain things stick with you. This was one of them. I guess you could say Walter was being sneaky, but I appreciated how well he knew me. He understood a direct approach wasn't going to work in that instance.

When I think about what the less direct route means, it's not taking a scenic route or meandering on your way.

It's about being flexible. It's about looking at a situation and seeing what's needed at the moment, not what logic may dictate, like drawing a straight line from point A to B. Instead, it's about understanding the people you're dealing with and figuring out what they need and what will work for them.

You may want to take the direct route. You may think you're helping someone by trying to make them do what you would do. In some instances, this might lead to a lot of frustration. You think you're helping, but the recipient of your help sees it as you doing you, not helping them in the way they need.

I have a friend who is a brilliant business owner. She runs multimillion-dollar projects, leads teams, and works with clients. She has an uncanny ability to see what's needed at the moment. She looks beyond the surface, sees behind what's obvious, to find what a team member or client actually wants to hear or get done. It's very often the less direct route that takes the project across the finish line. Her ability to see what's needed and her willingness to follow that path has made her extremely successful.

THE LESSON

The most direct approach won't always be the most effective. There are times when finding a subtler approach wins the day.

THE PRACTICE

Many of us have busy lives and we tend to move quickly from one task to the next. It's often easier to power through conversations and situations than to see the nuance and complexity that exist in all of us. It's usually only when the direct route doesn't work that we take a step back to figure out what happened. We tend to forget that how we operate best isn't necessarily best for everyone else. When working with other people, listen with awareness. Don't jump past what they're saying so you can speak. Listen with as much attention and presence as possible and without hurrying or pushing your agenda forward. This is a powerful way to look for what's needed in the moment.

WHAT HELPS

Slow down. Don't assume you know what's needed in any given situation. Take the time to truly listen not only to others but also to your own intuition and feelings.

40.

YOU NEVER KNOW WHAT SOMEONE GETS OUT OF A RELATIONSHIP

WHEN I WAS younger, I'd look at certain relationships and be mystified by one of the people involved in them. Walter was always there to remind me that what we see in public is often very different from how people are in private. He understood that one never knows, just from looking at the surface, what people get out of being together.

For instance, we may see a friend who is an extremely nice guy in a relationship with a very demanding and seemingly unkind woman. Yet he's devoted to her and their relationship. We think to ourselves, "Why does he stay? Why does he put up with it?" Of course, we see this in all combinations of people and it's not gender or orientation specific. Sometimes, we look at a relationship and we just don't understand why.

The truth I've learned is other people's relationships are not ours to judge or even to understand. The dynamics of a relationship are often not what they seem on the surface.

This goes for those relationships that look picture perfect, the ones that shock everyone around them when they end. What happens in private between people in a relationship can be very different from what the outside world sees.

Not only that, but we may often misread those dynamics as they present publicly. For example, Walter was very particular about the table he got when we'd go out to a restaurant. He didn't want to sit near the kitchen, he didn't want to sit outside if there was any ongoing traffic passing by, and he didn't want to sit near a wait station. It just became easier for me to manage the seating arrangements in restaurants because I was much less agitated about where we sat than he was. However, to the outside world, he was the quiet, laid-back one and I was the one making sure where we were seated was just right. On the surface, it appeared one way, but it was actually the opposite of what people saw. See what I mean? What it looks like on the outside and what it truly is can be different.

Personal relationships are the most intense mirrors for us. They reveal all our deepest insecurities and triggers. Some are meant to last only until we learn a particular lesson and then end. We may not understand the dynamics of our friends' or family members' other relationships, but as long as they don't cross the line into abuse, it's not our place to judge.

THE LESSON

While we care deeply about our friends, we should not judge their relationships. No one outside the relationship truly knows the full story of what goes on privately, nor what those in the relationship are learning or getting out of it.

THE PRACTICE

We are human and when we care for someone, we want the best for them. That means it can be impossible *not* to have an opinion about someone else's relationship. It can also feel impossible not to judge when we think someone's relationship is changing or influencing them in a way we don't like. Can you take a moment and imagine how you would feel if people close to you openly judged your relationship? How would that feel? Now imagine the people close to you made a point of letting you know they are there for you to support you however you need it. Which one feels better? Which one makes you feel closer to them? Treat others as you would like to be treated.

WHAT HELPS

We each have our own path to walk in this life. We have to trust that our friends and loved ones are learning what they need to learn through their relationship.

41.

WHATEVER YOU DON'T WORK OUT WITH ONE PARTNER, YOU'LL HAVE TO WORK OUT WITH THE NEXT

OVER HIS CAREER, Walter probably did well over ten thousand one-on-one readings. As you can imagine, he covered many different situations with people. One recurring topic was relationships. People would always ask Walter what they should do about their relationship: should they stay or should they go was the eternal question. While sometimes I could predict Walter's response to something, it was never a given. Just when I thought he'd go in one direction, he went in a totally opposite one.

It was the same thing when it came to relationships. I might look at a couple and think, "Oh heck yeah, those two people need to break up and get far away from each other!" However, if the couple was physically and emotionally safe, Walter would always ask them to take a deep dive into the relationship and assess why they wanted to end it. He knew that whatever issues someone thought they had with their partner, were most likely at least in part, their own issues too. He always told people they could leave the relationship, but they'd still have the same underlying issues to work out with their next partner. "Do you want to stay and work them out with the person you already know and love, or start all over again with someone new?" he'd ask. Now as you can imagine, context is everything, and everyone's response to this question was different. Some people chose to stay and work on the relationship, others decided to leave.

It can be easy for us to believe it's the other person. For instance, you may be thinking, "What if one of the people in the relationship has an addiction problem they aren't dealing with? How is that their partner's issue?" Well, why is someone attracted to someone with an addiction problem? What's going on with them? Maybe someone else's drama keeps them from having to focus on themselves. Maybe they feel responsible for healing their partners. Whatever the situation may be, there's some pattern that person will take and duplicate in the next relationship they have. It may manifest in a slightly different way, but it will keep coming up until the person decides to acknowledge and heal it.

Walter died when we were living in Portland, Oregon. It's a great city with much to offer. But it is the Pacific Northwest, which means it's grey and rainy often. The weather there really affects people. Over time, it became harder and harder for me to live there. When I moved to Denver, I was able to see what patterns in my life I was blaming on Portland and which ones were absolutely mine. The truth is, wherever you go, there you are. It was true for me when I moved and it's true for relationships too.

This isn't to say you should never leave a relationship, or go to extremes to try to make things work out. It does mean we humans are really good at the blame game. It's not us; it's them. But it's us too. Take a minute (or more) and try to figure out your part in why something is or isn't working.

THE LESSON
It's so easy to blame our relationship problems on other people. If they would just change, if they acted differently, everything would be fine. It's *never* just the other person. It's you too.

THE PRACTICE
When you feel ready to walk away from a relationship, ask yourself what patterns you may be taking with you. Can you give yourself the space to assess what you need to work on so you have more to offer your next partner? Seeing ourselves objectively is incredibly hard to do. Sometimes we need to work with someone to see our own patterns clearly.

WHAT HELPS
People are complicated, and relationships can be challenging. Have compassion for yourself and the person you're in a relationship with. Acknowledge that you co-create the relationship. When there are issues, it's not either/or, but both of you.

42.

HOW SOMEONE TALKS ABOUT OTHER PEOPLE IS HOW THEY'LL TALK ABOUT YOU

HUMANS ARE SOCIAL creatures. We like to share stories, and many people like to process their lives by talking to others. Seeking advice, describing our experiences, and looking for understanding can all be very constructive. At the other end of this stick are gossip and mean-spirited comments said behind someone's back. This behavior is destructive rather than constructive. Let's be honest, most of us at one time or another have gossiped about someone, either at work or maybe in a friend circle. We justify and rationalize it in many different ways.

I remember relaying to Walter something an acquaintance had said about a mutual friend. I thought it was funny. Walter didn't laugh at all. Instead, he said if that person is talking about your friend that way, it means she's talking about you the same way to other people. I was taken aback for a few moments. As I began to really think about it, I realized because of issues I was having with this friend, I was gleefully repeating a story that didn't paint them in a positive light. Not only that, but I also hadn't considered how someone talks about other people is how they'll talk about me to others. This was a big wake-up call for me and it changed how I behaved from that day forward.

While we have no control over how others talk about us, we do have control over how we talk about other people. We also have control over what we participate in with others. It's important to be as aware as possible about our intentions and motives when we find ourselves talking about other people. It can be easy to fall into the habit of complaining about others when they aren't around. However, you may be energetically draining the people you're complaining to with that negativity, even if they never say you are. Think about why you're talking about someone. Is it truly because you're trying to understand what's going on or need help figuring out how to handle a situation? Are you coming from a place of kindness? There's a lot to be said for keeping unkind and judgmental thoughts to yourself.

THE LESSON

How we talk about other people is a great opportunity to practice kindness and self-awareness. It's also an opportunity for us to think about how we're participating in conversations and whether that needs to change.

THE PRACTICE

First, we have to become aware of when and how we talk about someone when they aren't around. Second, we need to question our motives for the conversation. Do we need support and advice about a situation? Are we talking negatively about someone because they hurt our feelings or made us mad? This distinction may be subtle, but you know in your heart if you're lashing out or searching for understanding. This practice really comes down to bringing more attention and awareness to how we speak about others.

WHAT HELPS

Being conscientious about what we say about others is a long-term practice. We have to make it a priority. The gossip habit can be challenging to change if it's become a regular part of our lives. Changing our approach and behavior doesn't happen overnight. Make your best effort and start over as many times as you need to. Be kind to yourself because this is a process.

43.

WATCH WHAT PEOPLE DO, NOT WHAT THEY SAY

IF I COULD only take one life lesson from having known Walter, it would be to pay attention to people's actions rather than their words. When we first meet someone—whether it's a friend, co-worker, or possible love interest—we may be captivated by who they appear to be. Their humor may dazzle us, or we'll feel an instant connection and think, "Yes, a kindred spirit." We thoroughly enjoy being around them. As time goes on, though, we may begin to notice that their actions aren't in alignment with their words.

This is not to say people can't make mistakes or be imperfectly human. However, it takes time, sometimes years, before a person reveals who they truly are to us. We have to decide how close we let ourselves get to someone and how quickly; how much about ourselves we divulge and how emotionally vulnerable we allow ourselves to be. We do all of this while understanding we may not be seeing everything about who the person in front of us really is. In any close relationship we open ourselves to the full spectrum of feelings, all the risks and rewards. This is normal.

After Walter died, I met a wonderful friend, who really seemed to be a kindred spirit. We hung out often and stayed in contact daily through either texts or phone calls for a year. This person would make a point of telling me how we would be friends for the rest of our lives. Then, one day, this person ghosted me. There was no dramatic event, disagreement, or anything out the ordinary. I gave them space, confused at first. I soon realized there was no going back to what we had. I also remembered around the time we first started becoming friends that they had another friend who seemed desperate to connect, and yet they brushed that person off. In retrospect, I realize this person was a serial monogamist when it came to friendships. They would be close to one person, but then after an extended amount of time, they would be done and move on. As much as I thought I knew this person, I only knew the part they allowed me to see. Only over time did they reveal a larger part of who they are through their actions.

Of course, my feelings were hurt, but it was a good reminder too. It doesn't mean we don't take risks on people or that relationships don't change over time. It does mean we need to take care of ourselves in relationships with others. I know some people who aren't fazed by a person not turning out to be who they presented themselves to be. I know other people who would take it extremely hard. We can decide how we want to approach any relationship when we remember that we need to watch people's actions over time to get a true idea of who they are.

While some people purposely mislead others, most people may not even realize what they say and what they do don't match up. We have no control over others. We can only manage our response and care for ourselves by valuing who we are and understanding what we need from others. Relationships are a process and it takes time to see who someone truly is after the initial excitement fades away.

THE LESSON

People reveal who they are not by what they say, but through their actions over time.

THE PRACTICE

This practice asks us to become more aware about ourselves and how we operate in the world. For instance, do our own actions align with what we say? What expectations do we have about new relationships in our lives? Can we see what may motivate us to overlook someone's actions when they don't match what they say? The act of asking ourselves these questions opens us to a new awareness.

WHAT HELPS

Be mindful of words and actions not aligning. Don't be afraid to ask for clarification once there are too many unmatched words and actions. Remember that new relationships are exciting. We want to jump in pedal to the metal. There's nothing wrong with that. Often, though, we invest a lot of ourselves in new relationships, which can manifest in many different ways—emotionally, financially, or socially. What that new relationship appears to be and what it may end up being can be two entirely different things.

44.

FIND A PARTNER WHO BOTH LIKES AND LOVES YOU

FINDING A PARTNER who both likes and loves you is a piece of advice that came out of being married to Walter. We'd both experienced relationships where someone said they loved us, but they didn't necessarily like us. Relationships, especially over decades, will have challenging moments. Your partner will irritate you and you'll irritate them. If you begin a relationship where there is love, but underneath that love you don't really like the person or they don't really like you, you've got a hard road ahead. The same goes for liking someone but not really loving them.

The best way I can describe someone who loves but doesn't like you is if you have a partner who's always criticizing or disapproving of who you really are. An example of this would be if you've got an outgoing personality and they try to make you quiet down all the time. It also might feel like they are always trying to change who you are. At the same time, if you like a partner but don't really love them, you could end up feeling a bit martyred or victimized by the relationship.

In the throes of new love, we often overlook a lot. It never occurs to us how our future lives will be shaped by the partner we choose, especially a long-time partner. But your life will be affected by everything—from your partner's sociability quotient to their career prospects. Life and relationships throw a lot at us. Partnerships are always in flux. If you want to get the most out of a partnership, it definitely helps to be in one where you *both* like and love each other. If either partner is lacking one of these in the relationship, it's going to be that much more difficult for the relationship to thrive over time. It can be disappointing when we realize one of these elements isn't there. The relationship may have a lot to offer, but our best chance for fulfillment is when both exist if we're looking for a more long-term situation.

THE LESSON

When it comes to a loving relationship, you deserve to be both liked and loved for who you are. Sure, you're not perfect but no one is. Being both liked and loved by a partner is one of the delights of being human.

THE PRACTICE

We all need to decide what we want out of a relationship. No one can answer that question for you, and no one else can really understand what your partner does for you. Assess if you are in unhappy relationships but are scared to be alone. Or, are you so busy that it takes something like a pandemic to slow you down long enough to realize you aren't happy in a relationship? Making time to value and appreciate who you are is an important step in finding the relationship that works for you. Working on any issues you have around self-worth and stepping into your own sovereignty are good places to start this process.

WHAT HELPS

Be honest with yourself. Don't change who you are for anyone else. Be brave, be daring, and highly value who you are. Every relationship in your life reflects who you are, how you treat yourself, and what you expect from others.

45.

BE WITH SOMEONE YOU'RE NOT AFRAID TO GROW OLD WITH

RELATIONSHIPS ARE COMPLICATED. Over time, people change. In long-term relationships, we begin to see ourselves and our partners a little more clearly and better understand who our partner is and who we are together. We get to see what parts of ourselves we bring out in each other.

Of course, when we first fall in love, everything is new, exciting, and passionate. We overlook the mundane details of what it will be like to live and love together throughout the years. Realistically, it isn't always easy to predict the long-term course of any relationship because, hey, life happens.

With all this in mind, I can share a vital nugget of wisdom Walter gave me. If you end up being in a relationship with someone who is not nice to you, make a change. If you were to deal with a serious illness or just the normal issues that come with aging, how will your partner treat you? If your partner must step in and make decisions for you or becomes your caretaker, will they be kind? Will they have your back?

Or will they use your vulnerability (even if it's temporary) to act out their resentments and disappointments?

Let's face it, no one really wants to think of their partner in this way, but I'm sure some people know exactly what I'm talking about. They also know, deep down, whether there is cause to worry about how their partner would treat them if they couldn't physically or emotionally care for themselves.

I'll say it again: relationships are complicated. Your partner may love you, but how do they treat you? How do they treat themselves? Are they willing to adapt if necessary? I can tell you Walter would strongly urge you not to be with someone you're afraid to grow old with. If you are, it may be time to think about what needs to change in your life.

THE LESSON

The dynamics of a relationship can be delicate. If everything is going fine and everyone gets what they want, then all might be well. However, you must know what could happen when things aren't going well. In the face of struggles or illness when the power dynamic shifts more to one person, there should kindness and love, not anger and resentment.

THE PRACTICE

This is a tough one to think about. It cuts deeply into dealing with the dynamics of a relationship that we may have let slide. Someone may love us, and we may love them, but what patterns are in place and acted out? Does the love we have for someone translate to caring and kindness when they are most vulnerable, and vice versa? Take the time to look at how you and your partner(s) communicate with each other. Do you operate as a team when challenges come up between you to find a solution? Or do you pull away from each other and try to be right? If you sense there are underlying issues no one wants to tackle, you may consider getting professional help to clear the air and tend to the long-term health of your relationship.

WHAT HELPS

Value and trust yourself. When you learn to treat yourself with true kindness and gentleness, you will be able to give and receive the same to others. One way to begin to develop this trust is through meditation. Sitting quietly, noticing how you feel and accepting yourself exactly as you are is a great starting point.

46.

WHEN YOU LOVE, LOVE COMPLETELY

MY HUSBAND WASN'T a millionaire or a celebrity, but when we got together, I felt like I had won the lottery. What can I say? He made me happy. It's funny how we have certain memories that imprint themselves on our being and stay with us forever. One of those for me was a conversation Walter and I had early on in our relationship. I don't remember why it came up or any of the circumstances around it. What I do remember is Walter saying, "One thing that you will always be able to count on is that at the end of your life, you will know absolutely that you were truly and completely loved."

Whenever I think about this, I tear up, no matter how many years it's been since Walter died. He gave me the most amazingly precious gift by not only saying this to me, but also living it with me every day. I always knew without a doubt that he loved me. We annoyed each other and argued at times, but I don't think either of us ever doubted we were well and truly loved by the other. We were each other's biggest supporters and advocates.

Loving someone as fully and completely as you can is a tremendous gift both for yourself and others. It may require you to dig into your own self-development to get past any inner barriers that keep you from being available to love someone. It may take work and courage because love can be scary and make us feel vulnerable. We may have been hurt before and felt the pain of a broken heart. Whatever has happened in the past, in this moment there's a new opportunity to open our hearts to others.

There's an old movie called *Ghost* that stars Demi Moore and Patrick Swayze. At the very end of the movie, Swayze's character (spoiler alert: he's dead) says, "It's amazing. The love inside, you take it with you." What I've experienced is just that. The love you're given always stays with you. Walter died, but the love he gave me is still with me. I can feel it. He was right when said at the end of this life I will know—because I do know—I was l truly and completely loved by someone else. What is more important in life than finding your ability to love and sharing that love with other people?

THE LESSON

Let yourself love the people in your life fully. It's a gift for you and them.

THE PRACTICE

I know a couple who always says, "I love you" to each other whenever either of them leaves the other. It doesn't matter if it's a quick trip to the grocery store, a workday, or a longer trip. They make a point of always expressing their love every day no matter what. Find a way every day to tell people you love them either through your words or actions. Whether you're single or in a partnership, consider starting a gratitude jar. Leave little love notes to yourself or another person in the jar about what you're grateful for, what you appreciate, or what you love.

WHAT HELPS

Loving others starts with loving ourselves. Feeling deeply or letting go of fear or insecurity are inside jobs. We have to be willing to put the time into our own personal development to deepen our relationship with ourselves in order to be able to love others.

47.

HONOR YOUR LOVED ONE'S PATH

ONE OF THE most difficult lessons I learned during Walter's cancer diagnosis and the last thirteen months of his life was to honor the path his life was taking. The more I understood the seriousness of his diagnosis, the more I wished I were the terminal one, not him. I think anyone who has witnessed a loved one fight a disease understands the helplessness of watching their struggle and not being able to take on that fight directly. Walter was such an amazing spiritual teacher, and part of me really wanted to take on his illness so he could stay here and continue his work.

Along with chemo and radiation, Walter also had weekly acupuncture sessions. I would drive him to his appointment and sometimes I would do a session myself or sit in the waiting room. Every day was a struggle for me, knowing my favorite person in the world was losing his fight and wouldn't be here much longer. I found myself sitting alone quietly crying, not understanding why him and not me instead. One time, his acupuncturist happened to walk by and did a double-take as he passed the waiting room and saw me crying. Normally, I tried to put on a good face, joke around, and be optimistic. He very kindly took the time to come in and find out what was going on with me. As I explained that I wished I could take on Walter's illness so he could continue being an amazing teacher and help more people, he stopped me mid-sentence. "Don't you see by doing that you dishonor his path?" I was taken aback because… what? I was dishonoring Walter? The acupuncturist continued, "This is his pathway to walk, not yours. Yours is different. You need to honor that this is the course his life is taking; this is his experience to learn from, not yours. That's not something you can do for someone else. Honor him by letting him walk down the path in front of him."

This five-, maybe ten-minute conversation completely changed my perspective. It was exactly what I needed to hear at that moment. I realized how true this was about so many things we see in relationships with others. If we love someone who is dealing with addiction, for example, that's not something we can take from them or make better for them. They must walk down that path and find the way themselves. There's only so much we can do for our loved ones. Sometimes all we can do, no matter how painful it may be to us, is to stand by them and watch as they walk their own path. We honor them by holding the space and standing back, realizing what's theirs to do for themselves and what's ours to do for ourselves.

THE LESSON

We can't live out someone else's life for them. It may be difficult to do, but when we stand by and witness their path in this world, we are honoring them with a huge amount of love.

THE PRACTICE

It's so tempting to want to take on a loved one's pain and difficulties. We would often rather suffer something ourselves than watch them suffer. When facing such a circumstance, what I can offer as a practice is sitting quietly with open hands. Listen to the sound of your breath. As you're able to, let your breath lengthen and deepen and let your hands rest in front of you, palms facing up. Keep your hands open. There is nothing to change, there is nothing to fix, there is no other way you need to be. Let yourself feel the deep acceptance of your open hands.

WHAT HELPS

Remember each of us has come into this world to learn and experience different things, no matter how wonderful or difficult. Our path is ours to walk and embrace. We honor each other by supporting that journey no matter what it looks like and by not trying to take over someone else's experience.

48.

RELATIONSHIPS GO
ON AFTER DEATH

WHEN WALTER DIED, people would say to me, "You know he's still with you in spirit. He'll always be with you. So really it's like he's there." I know this was meant to be comforting and they were trying to be helpful, but this 100 percent did not help me. In movies and television when ghosts or spirits make themselves known, it's supposed to somehow ease the pain of grief. They're not really gone, they're just in a different place. There's probably someone out there who would find this thought comforting, but I did not. The person who Walter was, the physical embodiment of that person, did, of course, die. His death left a gaping hole in my life and heart.

The truest thing I can share about the death of a loved one is that, for me, time itself did indeed heal that wound. It wasn't a linear progression and there were no stages, but healing did happen. The other thing I can share is your relationship with a loved one who dies doesn't end with their death. We can debate whether there's an afterlife or whether spirits actually contact you from the other side; but as Walter and I used to say to each other, let's not and say we did. Instead, I'll say I believe relationships go on after death because at a certain point, when you're a little less sad, you start to think about the person who died and smile. You see something you wish you could tell them about and you think, "Oh, how they would have loved it," and you smile at that too.

Relationships go on after death because you keep the memory of that person alive in your heart. You tell them things or laugh about how they would have hated something you're doing or something you bought. Their life on this physical plane may have ended, but you take them with you into the rest of your life because the love you shared still lives inside of you. No one and nothing can take away what you shared. Those experiences remain with you throughout your life.

I always wished Walter would have written wisdom-filled letters to me like the main character in the movie *P. S. I Love You*. In that movie, the wife goes on a healing journey after her husband's death through a series of letters he left for her. Yeah, that didn't happen for me. I didn't find any secret notes from Walter telling me I'd be okay. But over time, I've had the sense he's watching out for me and making sure I'm okay more and more. It feels like I have a great, big, personal guardian angel watching over me. He may not be here with me in the way he was before, but, in my heart and spirit, I know we will always be connected.

THE LESSON

When people are alive, love them with all your heart. When people die, still love them with all your heart.

THE PRACTICE

Loss and grief are profound emotions that can shake the foundations of our lives. Everyone processes grief differently and there's no one right way to do it. If it feels right for you, consider keeping a journal where you tell the loved one about your day or week. Write an annual letter letting them know how you're doing. Find ways that work for you to remember your loved one who died and honor that relationship.

WHAT HELPS

As you begin to heal, you may miss the physical presence of the person who has died, but over time, you will find that they live on in your heart. You can talk to them and smile at the memories you have, and even think about what they'd have to say about your life now.

49.

FIERCELY PROTECT YOUR BELIEF
IN YOUR WORK AND YOURSELF

WALTER DIDN'T EVER directly talk about self-belief, but he lived it every day. If you think it was easy for a regular guy from Philly, who spent years on his education and thought he'd be an English professor, to instead work as a clairvoyant, you'd be wrong.

To be a spiritual teacher and run a meditation center, Walter had to let go of how he thought his life would turn out. He also had to believe in himself and the work he was doing completely. Walter ended up in a profession some people hold in low regard. Those same people felt it was okay to belittle his work as a psychic and spiritual teacher. I never once saw Walter waver in his belief in himself or his work. Yes, not everything worked out perfectly because no one's life does. Still, the words that come to mind when I think of his approach to his work and belief in himself, are "fiercely protective."

No matter what your goals and dreams are in life, there will always be outside influences that either directly or indirectly discourage you. We often look to others for support and direction. We want someone else to tell us we're doing the right thing and are on the right track. When it comes to our own hopes and desires, it's important to recognize that while support from others is great, we must be the ones who fiercely protect our tender, hopeful dreams. It doesn't matter if those dreams are about love, relationships, work, or hobbies. We must be our own protectors, keeping the hopes of our vulnerable inner selves safe.

In particular, I remember a time when Walter was working with a woman who booked speakers for large events. She booked him to speak to a group of people in the travel industry. Both the agent and I encouraged him to get out there and look at it as a great opportunity. We were optimistic about it. Walter accepted the booking, even though he felt it was the wrong venue for him. He was absolutely right; it was a terrible fit. After that, he absolutely would not do an event he didn't feel aligned with his work. He'd been willing to try it because he had two people who, let's face it, were pressuring him to take the opportunity. The booking agent continued to suggest events that weren't a fit even though they often appeared to be great opportunities. Walter stood by what he knew was best for him and never did another event he felt wasn't right for him. He didn't care how great the opportunity looked on paper.

It is easy to think we are already committed to following our dreams. However, there's a difference between commitment and deep down in our bones nurturing and protecting of our essential, creative selves. Walter taught me you must be intentional when protecting the pursuit of your goals from outside naysayers and your own self-sabotaging voices.

You need to be passionately committed to being your own advocate in life. Not in a negative way, but in a fiercely strong, nurturing, and loving way.

THE LESSON
Fiercely protect your hopes, dreams, and creative essential self.

THE PRACTICE
Our dreams and creative selves are tender things that can make us feel vulnerable at times. Can you truly feel and understand the value of your particular point of view in this life? Your uniqueness is expressed in this world through your hopes, dreams, and creativity. Be determined to value and protect what's yours to give in this life. One of the ways you can do this is to prioritize your own self-development. Make time to explore your inner world to discover more of who you are and what you are here to give this world. Set aside time each day to do your inner work.

WHAT HELPS
We can be incredibly casual about our hopes and dreams. We work toward them, but then we can also be easily influenced and sometimes tossed about like waves in a storm by others opinions and life's circumstances. Be fiercely protective of your creative self and nurture it so it grows strong and untouched by outside influences.

50.

YOU ARE YOUR OWN BEST TEACHER

WALTER TAUGHT ME the spiritual philosophy of being my own best teacher. I'm sure he came to this himself from existing philosophies and his own experience as a clairvoyant medium. Almost all the spiritual pathways I've studied share similar principles with a slightly different flavor of perspective and truth.

Self-teaching trusts that you are your own best teacher. It empowers you to learn from everything and everyone around you, knowing they are mirroring back what you need to see. It asks you to trust your inner voice and authority. Being your own best teacher means having faith in yourself, even when others may not. This doesn't mean you don't ask for advice or have other teachers. It does mean that when you develop a relationship with your higher being and inner world, you become the ultimate authority in your life. You understand you are the framer and maker of your own reality.

It's easy for us to get wrapped up in the distractions of this world and let our own personal development work fall by the wayside. If, however, we pay attention and stay awake to the present moment, we will begin to see patterns emerge. Those patterns are our personal lessons and mythology. When we commit to and trust our own spiritual pathway, then we realize everything we need is already inside of us because we live in an interconnected universe.

Ultimately, I feel being your own teacher means not giving your power away carelessly or unconsciously. It's understanding that you and something sacred deep within are the ultimate decision makers when it comes to who you are and how you will live your life.

THE LESSON

You are the teacher you need in this world.

THE PRACTICE

If you choose to be your own teacher, then you've decided to embark on a journey of spiritual self-discovery and development. It is a work of a lifetime. It never ends and it will always be an imperfect practice. Here are some of the elements that you can incorporate into your life to help take you on this mission:

- Make space for daily mindful awareness and meditation
- Practice compassion and non-judgment
- Embrace the interconnectedness of the universe
- Strive for moderation in all things
- Trust yourself
- Be of service to others

WHAT HELPS

Being a spiritual being having a human adventure can be quite the challenge. There will be times when the journey is glorious and others when it is gut-wrenching. I do not believe there is any mission we can take on more worthy of our dedication than finding our way back to wholeness and our larger spiritual source.

ABOUT THE AUTHOR

Writer, consultant, and educator, Mary-Frances Makichen developed a passion for helping people navigate times of change after going through a series of changes herself, including the passing of her late husband, Walter. She thoroughly enjoys using her intuitive and emotional intelligence to help people learn to trust themselves and connect with their own inner teacher.

Mary-Frances has been featured on The Huffington Post and Tiny Buddha, and she's now the host of the popular podcast, "You've Got This." You can get tips about mindfulness, resilience, power, and belonging by signing up for her newsletter at maryfrancesmakichen.com or following her on Instagram @mfmakichen.

Made in the USA
Las Vegas, NV
06 October 2021

31844238R00125